FOOD
FOR THE
SPIRIT

Seasonal Vegetarian Recipes
to Warm the Kitchen
and Nourish the Soul

By Manuela Dunn Mascetti and Arunima Borthwick

Daybreak™ Books
An Imprint of Rodale Books
New York, New York

Cover Designer: Jane Colby Knutila
Cover Illustrator: Pamela Rossi
Book Designer: Faith Hague

Library of Congress Cataloging-in-Publication Data

Mascetti, Manuela Dunn.
     Food for the spirit: seasonal vegetarian recipes to warm the kitchen and nourish the soul / by Manuela Dunn Mascetti and Arunima Borthwick.
       p.   cm.
     Includes bibliographical references and index.
     ISBN 0–87596–460–5 hardcover
     1. Vegetarian cookery. 2. Food—Religious aspects. I. Borthwick,
     Arunima. II. Title.
    I. Borthwick, Arunima. II. Title.
    TX837.D86   1998
    641.5'636—dc21   97–23758

Distributed in the book trade by St. Martin's Press

2 4 6 8 10 9 7 5 3 1   hardcover

For
Osho

*[Babette] had the ability to transform a dinner into
a kind of love affair. A love affair that made no distinction
between bodily appetite and spiritual appetite...*
—Isak Dinesen, from *Babette's Feast*

CONTENTS

Part II. *Right* Food, *Right* Eating

ACKNOWLEDGMENTS

THIS BOOK WOULD NEVER HAVE BEEN BORN had it not been for the gentle but persistent encouragement of our English publisher, Michael Alcock. He was the first to recognize the "soul quality" of our candlelit dinners and to offer his enthusiastic support throughout the conception and the writing. Thank you for fathering this creation into life.

We also want to express our gratitude to Karen Kelly of Daybreak Books, who saw and understood the value of combining diet with mindfulness to create spiritual well-being; she is an inspired editor who believes in her authors' projects and provides support throughout the birth of the book.

Thank you to Faith Hague and Jane Knutila for creating a work of elegant beauty; their design graces the pages you now hold. Thank you to Linda Mooney and Kathryn A. Cressman, our copy editors, who contributed accuracy and improved the structure of the text to make this a better book.

The enchanted world of Osho is the true spirit that blesses this work. Sitting with Him in meditation and spending time in His beautiful commune in Pune, India, is what has truly enabled the flower He gave us to shed its fragrance in our daily lives. Our deep gratitude is to Him and to all those sannyasis who continue undaunted in the work He set before us.

Thank you to the Osho International Foundation for allowing us to enrich the text with Osho's original words and meditations.

And, finally, thank you to P and M for loving us more every day.

INTRODUCTION

Practice random acts of kindness
And senseless acts of beauty.
—Anne Herbert

IN THE TIME OF THE INDIAN SAINT MAHAVIRA, his Jain monks would sweep the path before them with brooms, and they would do this whenever they walked because they believed that every living thing, plant or animal, was a soul waiting to be reincarnated into human consciousness; to kill it by mistake, to kill it unconsciously, was to interfere with its karmic process. The Jain attitude to nonviolence underscores an enchantment with the world: If the world has a soul, then the world is a soul mate and a lover, and thus it is part of ourselves.

As children we were read fairy tales—the main characters of which were animals leading real lives parallel to our own. The enchantment of childhood is in believing that everything outside us is like us, alive and inhabited by a soul. The awe and respect for the world that childhood and sainthood share become distorted when our thoughts and actions fail to respect not only that vital bond with our environment but fail to care for our bodies also. Eating is ingesting parts of the world. If this was firmly lodged in our memories when we set out to prepare a meal, imagine what kind of food we would choose. Perhaps we would not want to eat anything that resulted from killing. Instead, we might choose products that were naturally derived from the earth.

Throughout Asian countries, from India to Thailand, certain days are dedicated to sharing the bounty of the earth with all its living forms. Traditionally vegetarian, Asia honors the abundance of the planet in thousands of ways every day of the year.

This book is an invitation to participate in the sacred dimension of cooking and eating the bounty that Nature offers us. Blessed as we are with plenty, we can feast every day with an extraordinary array of produce that has been organically grown to respect the environment and to protect us from the harmful effects of pesticides and chemical fertilizers.

Within these pages there is also an open invitation for all of us to start caring for our planet in the same way we care for our bodies, in whatever small or grand ways we can practically manage. We are now in the latter quarter of the twentieth century, when half of humanity appears to be dying from starvation and the other half seems to be choking on its own excess, and we are, individually, largely unaware of this condition and its effects on the planet.

Many of the recipes and the principles behind this book originate from temple life. Having spent years living in ashrams and communes, where the main focus is meditation, we feel that food that has been cultivated and prepared with awareness and love, with no expectation for personal gain, is the best food to nourish the spirit. Cooking with natural ingredients is a way of contemplating beauty and of offering a work of beauty to others—this is the giving and receiving that adds depth to everyday life.

We suggest that you create a temple out of your kitchen, too. Take the time that you spend there, whether you're making breakfast or simply preparing a cup of tea, as your time of spiritual retreat. Be slow and gentle, and pay attention to what you do and how you do it. The more meditative you are in your approach to nourishment, the less stressed and the more healed you will be—this is a natural and simple equation that does not fail. Allow your intuition and imagination to help you play with food and with the serving of your meals. No matter how tired or restless you may feel when you are about to start your cooking tasks, if your kitchen is a temple, you will feel renewed and re-enchanted by your time spent there.

We hope that you will enjoy these recipes and the meditations offered in this book. Above all, we hope that you, too, will gain insight into the sacredness of small gestures in everyday tasks.

Part I

MAKING
THE BODY *A*
TEMPLE

Chapter 1

RELIGION, MAGIC, RITUAL, AND FOOD

THE SACRED DIMENSION of preparing and eating food has been eclipsed in our homes, and yet these are actions that we perform daily, just like rituals in temples. We are fortunate, indeed, not only in being able to eat every day but also in being able to choose from an incredible abundance of produce. Yet we must remember that our lives are very different from that of a million others who are starving as we are eating. It is not the precious nature of food that makes it sacred, although this has been a major influence in the past. Sacredness is a certain way of caring for what we eat and how we eat. It reveals attention, healing, value, and heart. We do not use the word *sacred* in a religious context; it is rather a quality or a dimension of experiencing everyday actions. Valuing the sacredness of food means eating soulfully, which in turn implies that particular attention is given to what we choose to take from the outside in order to nourish the inside. In this simple osmosis we can either feel a sense of relating to the whole or we can carry on the process automatically. The difference between these two attitudes is simple: a balance of health and harmony in the body, mind, and spirit.

All eating can be seen as communion, feeding the soul as well as the body. Our cultural habit of opting for fast food reflects our current belief that all we need to ingest is, both literally and figuratively, any food, not food of real substance shared with others in celebration at the dinner table. Most of our culture and science, physical and social, operates as if there were no interior life or at least assumes that the interior life has little or nothing to do with the outside world. When the interior is acknowledged, it is almost invariably regarded as secondary, to be attended to only after the business at hand of office, family, and home. The contemporary philosopher Thomas Moore says, "Culturally, we have a plastic esophagus, suited perhaps to fast food and fast living, but not conducive to the soul, which thrives only when life is taken in a long, slow process of digestion and absorption."

Retrieving the sacred in our lives demands that we bring back enchantment into everyday actions and processes. Enchantment in our surroundings, for instance, can be found if we begin to think in terms of having a house for our bodies, a home for our hearts, and a temple for our souls. The building—the place where we live—remains the same, but under the spell of enchantment, it is perceived as nurturing three very different, albeit equally important, functions. The same enchantment can be brought back to cooking and eating—these can be seen as the two magical functions of nourishing and healing our bodies. The kitchen then becomes a temple where, magically, raw food is alchemically transformed into a glorious substance that sustains us in all dimensions.

The author Isak Dinesen, in her famous tale *Babette's Feast*, tells us how Babette, an apparently simple French cook in the service of two old Danish sisters, spends money won in a lottery to buy the most expensive food for a celebration dinner in honor of the sisters' late father. As a preacher, their father had transformed, with his eloquent sermons and self-less dedication, the lives of all the members of the congregation who, upon his sudden death, feel abysmally lost and unguided. As the guests sit down for dinner, we get a sense of the bitterness of their lives; nothing is happy, the joyous taste has left their spirits. Babette, who is revealed to be quite a sorceress, not only serves an outstanding meal, but her cooking has the power to transform the quality of the guests' hearts. It is as though they were eating the essence of the parishioner and so, progressively, they absorb his enlightenment into their bodies during the meal. At the end of the evening, everyone feels pervaded by spiritual goodness, and they leave the house wondering whether they have been transmuted into angels. Their transformation is symbolic of the rite of the Eucharist, in which the communicant is purified as the divine essence—in the form of blessed food—is digested.

Babette's Feast is a richly woven tale that imaginatively describes the transformational power of food, but many more examples can be found in popular folk traditions. The witch's brew, the magic cauldron, the enchanted potion, the healing drink, the shaman's herbs for vision questing—these are all expressions of the timeless knowledge that food is not only for the body but it also essentially nourishes the soul. Britain and most of Asia have little else in common except for the daily ritual of tea. Tea, the inhabitants of these very different countries say, warms you when you are feeling cold, cools you when you are hot, calms you when you are agitated, and lifts you up when you are feeling down. A cup of tea means a moment of quiet and peace; as one sips, a sense of "ahness" pervades the mind, the body, and the spirit and a state of grace seems to descend. The ritual of tea can be seen as a very modest and small form of spiritual retreat: We are being there, quietly doing nothing except contemplating, in the goodness of the moment. These simple pleasures are where we cultivate the sense of the sacred every day.

The Ritual of Eating Together

Sitting together around a table for meals is far more than a practical necessity. In its sacral character the sharing of food and drink is probably the most ancient ritual of mankind. All societies celebrate rites of passage in this way. In Western and Christian examples, food is the centerpiece of Thanksgiving, Christmas, weddings, funerals, Irish wakes, and birthday parties. Eating together binds us in celebration.

The religious philosopher Thomas Merton summarized the ritual of communal eating beautifully in his book *The Living Bread*: "A feast is of such a nature that it draws people to itself and makes them leave everything else in order to participate in its joys. To feast together is to bear witness to the joy one has at being with his friends. The mere act of eating together, quite apart from a banquet or some other festival occasion, is by its very nature a sign of friendship and of communion."

In modern times, we have lost sight of the fact that even the most ordinary actions of our everyday lives are invested, by their very nature, with deep spiritual meaning. The table is in a certain sense the center of family life, the expression of family life.

So, too, with a banquet. The Latin word *convivium* contains more of this mystery than our words *banquet* and *feast*. To call a feast a convivium is to call it a mystery of the sharing of life—a mystery in which guests partake of the good things prepared and given to them by their host, and in which the atmosphere of friendship and gratitude expands into a sharing of thoughts and sentiments and ends in common rejoicing.

This mystery occurs in everyday life not only when we serve and share beautifully prepared food but also when we enhance the atmosphere around our table. When people eat together, they may be actually together in spirit or they may be far apart from one another. Some rooms invite people to eat leisurely and comfortably and feel together, while others force people to eat as quickly as possible so that they can go somewhere else to relax.

In order to enhance the intensity of feeling and well-being, you need to make your table the center of the room. Casting a pool of light over those who are sitting around the table draws everyone together, enclosing them within a circle. Leave the walls or surrounding area darker to accentuate the intimacy. Ideally, the table should be round as we relax far more when we sit at an angle from another person—conversation comes easily and we are able to deepen the bond. If you have a rectangular table, experiment with enclosing it in some kind of a circle, perhaps with shelves and counters for things related to the meal. Decorate your table with the beauty of the seasons; pin autumn leaves around the tablecloth and scatter berries between the plates, or ask your children to make garlands of fresh flowers for a light summer supper. Candles work miracles for winter evenings; they bring warmth and magic when outside is cold and dark. You will feel more satisfied when your meals are shared in the spirit of communion and celebration, with laughter, joy, and beauty accompanying good food.

The Magical Kitchen

Spirituality is seeded, germinates, sprouts, and blossoms in our kitchens, too. The kitchen has been regarded throughout history as a place of enchantment: This is where the hearth and the heart of the house are. In fact, kitchens help us transform a house into a home.

Modern architects of the recent past designed kitchens that were isolated from the rest of the house, even far away from the eating area. This is a holdover from the days of servants and sculleries in rich manor houses of the nineteenth century, when the rich ate in the dining room and the smells of cooking never permeated the main house. Anyone cooking in isolation will unconsciously feel like a servant far away "in the kitchen," as though the preparation of food were of less worth than the consumption of it and as though cooking were a chore rather than a pleasure. This is a position that is both unacceptable and unworkable. There exists an ancient psychological pattern within us that awakens to magic when food is being prepared and eaten; we naturally gather around the cooking stove, taste morsels of the food that is being made, and talk from the heart. This is a time and place that needs to be honored in our own homes.

As far as it is possible, make your kitchen like a cherished farmhouse kitchen found in very old homes and fairy tales, where family activity and the preparation of food are completely integrated. Ideally, the central piece is an old wooden table: Here is where members of the family talk, sit down after work, eat, and play cards and where small work of all kinds happens, like weaving wreaths for autumn and winter home decorations, painting homemade pottery, sewing, or decorating cakes and pies. The kitchen work can be done communally, both on the table and on the proper food counters along the walls. There might even be a comfortable old chair, maybe a rocking chair, where someone, a grandparent or a cat, can sleep through the activities. The chairs around the table may have been collected serendipitously and may be of different shapes to accommodate different people. The kitchen should be a bright and comfortable room, a room of memories where family history is woven in dream time. Maybe there are glass jars and pots containing grains, legumes, home-baked biscuits, and jams and other goods along exposed shelves. Plants are important, too, as are herbs, and maybe there is a corner where these are grown in terra-cotta vases.

More problems are solved and joys celebrated in the kitchen than in any other part of the house. It is here where we become alchemists every day and transform, like Babette in the tale, raw ingredients into food for the soul. It is also a place for meditation. As we cut vegetables, peel potatoes, choose what foods to cook, or watch water come to a boil, we gain a taste of silence and of being "in the moment." The enchantment is also to be found in all the kitchen utensils we use for cooking, and it is nurtured in the way we prepare meals. We all have favorite pots that cook better than any other, no matter how old or battered they are; or certain peelers, knives, or glasses that hold a special kind of magic that works again and again. Paying attention to the magic that is at work in the kitchen is an art—cooking soulfully—which may be enriched by the memory of a past when food was indeed sacred.

The first altar of mankind was the primitive hearth, a white mound of tightly packed ashes that kept the fire from dying. This is where the tribe gathered, seeking sanctuary from a world of darkness and predators, to weave tales of hunting exploits and to honor their guardian spirits. The white of the ashes was maintained as the color of temples throughout antiquity, and it came to be associated with purity. Interestingly, many of our modern kitchens are still white today. If we lift the veils of history to uncover how our ancestors regarded food, we may be surprised to learn that although time has passed, some aspects of life have been maintained.

The Prehistoric Diet

The connection between food and religion is extremely ancient, dating back to when the early Indo-European nomadic tribes came to settle, over centuries, in small communities and turned from violent hunters into more peace-loving gatherers. The need to grow food, rather than hunt for it, marked the beginning of civilization, as the agrarian lifestyle fostered stability in population growth, technological advancement, and social complexity. Religious art, ritual objects, carvings, and archaeological remains dating from that period help us define the image of existence as it was then: life-sustaining, nature-worshipping communities of men and women whose intimate relationship with the earth was paramount to their survival.

Far and wide in the geography of the sacred, we find temples, sanctuaries, and other religious structures erected as early as the Neolithic period to map the movements of the sun and moon and their influence upon the crops. Ancient places such as Stonehenge and Avebury in England are important psychic records of a time when people—lacking our scientific knowledge but possessing powerful mystical intuition and wisdom—tried to explain, study, and influence the cycles of nature. Their survival depended almost exclusively upon successful harvests, and this vital bond created a mystical participation with the earth from which their daily food was derived. There are many religious myths, spanning a huge period of time and landscape, that explicitly place agriculture and farming as the hallowed bond between the divine and mankind: Food is life and thus it is sacred. Food was offered to the gods upon these ancient altars, and it was placed within burial sites to sustain the departed in their journey to the other world. The need to find fertile plains determined where the greatest civilizations flowered.

Primitive cities acquired power by being able to store food and prevent threats such as famine, disease, and marauding tribes from annihilating them. The storage of food in Egypt and ancient Babylon was presided over by priests who also studied the movements of the sun and moon and were able to make accurate predictions on the outcome of forthcoming harvests. Syrius, the star thought to influence the waters of the Nile, was worshipped as a divinity as its visibility in the sky at a certain time of the year marked the flooding of the great river, which made the fields of Egypt fertile and guaranteed the survival of the land of pharaohs.

The great urban civilizations of Mesopotamia—Babylon, Sumer, and Assyria—which developed in Asia Minor nearly 5,000 years ago, and the reputedly even more ancient settlements of Old Europe have left us with a legacy that is relevant to us today: the primitive diet. It mainly consisted of grains such as wheat, barley, corn, millet, farmed vegetables, and legumes, which were regarded as sacred gifts from Mother Earth. This simple but nourishing diet has been the staple of mankind for millennia. It included little meat as most proteins and other nutrients are contained in grains and legumes. This stable combination was sustained throughout history; the universal commonality of the grinding stones found amidst archaeological remains of prehistoric villages shows us that grains formed the basis of all meals in the past. From the Celts to the Aztecs, from the ancient Egyptians to the classical Greeks, from the Native Americans to the African tribes—they all grew, harvested, ground, and cooked grains every day of their lives. The maintenance of a grain-based diet is further supported by the first written history of our own culture: Rome survived on its wheat and barley, on which even the conquering legions were fed. Medieval annals report that people throughout Europe ate mostly grains and some vegetables; ancient monastery records from France, Italy, and Germany again inform us that grains, wild herbs, and vegetables appeared at the refectory table. Northern Italian dishes such as risotto, polenta, and pasta e fagioli, which are very fashionable today, formed the grain-based winter diet of farmers and peasants for many centuries since the ingredients were both cheap and warmth-inducing. The thought that the race of mankind has been sustained on this diet for nearly 7,000 years is staggering. Today, the people of Asia are still nourished by daily bowls of rice.

In fact, the two different attitudes towards life and death, the cornerstones of human existence, are essentially dietary, explains Joseph Campbell in his authoritative study of the world's mythologies called *The Masks of God*. People whose nutrition is based upon the fruits of the Earth have over millennia come to feel a deep bond and respect for nature, and they view human existence as nonviolent and as following the same cycle as plants: birth, life, death, and rebirth. This attitude is now predominantly Eastern, as Asian people are mostly vegetarian and have a deep faith in this "eternal return," which is mirrored in their religion and mythology. People who kill in order to eat may often regard existence as being essentially brutal and violent: birth, life, and death, which is inevitably followed by the punishment of hell or eternal torment inflicted by vindictive ghosts and spirits. This view has been adopted by the West and is reflected in its monotheistic religions—Christianity, Judaism, and Islam—which are based upon the struggle between good and evil and which do not believe in the concept of the reincarnation of the soul.

It is this long-established habit of eating grains, legumes, and vegetables that makes it the ideal diet for our bodies; our digestive systems have been shaped on this staple for many thousands of years. Macrobiotic, Ayurvedic, Chinese, and other methods of healing by use of certain foods are based upon this diet. If in the West we have departed from this way of

The Miracle of Rice

- Rice is the most nutritious cereal grain.
- White rice contains just 82 calories per half-cup and brown rice only 89.
- Rice is cholesterol and gluten-free, low in sodium, and nonallergenic.
- People in Asia depend upon it for between 30 and 70 percent of their daily calories.
- More than 91 percent of the world's paddy (unmilled, rough rice) is grown and consumed there by half of the world's population.
- The largest paddy producers in the world are China, India, and Indonesia. They produce and consume more than 60 percent of all the world's rice.
- The average Asian consumes 200 pounds or more of rice per year, while the average European consumes less than 10 pounds.
- The United States' total yearly production of rice, just more than 7 million tons, would not fill the rice bowls of China for two weeks. Total U.S. exports would not feed tiny Nepal for a year.
- Today, 2.7 billion people rely on rice as their daily food staple. By 2025, the rice-dependent population could reach 3.9 billion.
- Asia's densely populated lands cannot, for the most part, afford to raise cattle. More than 90 percent of China's usable land is needed for crops. China manages to feed 20 percent of the world's population on less than 7 percent of the world's arable land.
- Asia has no more land available to plant more rice. Newer varieties of rice better fitted to the ecological systems where they grow need to be found in order to combat starvation in the next millennium.
- The International Rice Research Institute (IRRI) in Los Baños, Philippines, has engineered more than 250 new rice varieties that are now planted in 106 countries.

eating, it is only because the abundance of fast foods and ready-made meals has progressively confused our instinct about nutrition over the last three decades. Technology, while gifting us with plenty, has also contributed to the abstraction of the idea of food. As we no longer cultivate what we eat, it removes us further and further away from the original source of food. We now read on the back of packaging about its provenance and its chemical components. Baking our own bread is an entirely different experience than buying it already sliced and shrink-wrapped at an anonymous counter in a superstore. When we return to the original way of eating, something happens to our interiors; we suddenly discover the soul of food that emerges when we cook with the basic ingredients that have been used for thousands of years.

Today, when we visit Thai, Japanese, Indian, or Chinese restaurants, we not only gain an experience of a different way of eating but we also return to the essential and most healthy diet for our bodies. Asian countries, financially less affluent than our own, have maintained this ancient way of eating because the average household can afford to feed many on grains, legumes, and vegetables. Meat, fish, and sweets are still luxuries to be eaten only on special occasions. A number of modern diseases and health afflictions, such as allergies, candida yeast infections, diabetes, digestive disorders, heart disease, low and high blood pressure, hyperactivity in children, and many types of cancer, have been proven to be both prevented and cured by this form of diet.

Of all the ways of eating, this is the most spiritual diet for mankind; it is ancient and it balances mind, body, and soul in a way that no other food combination does. This is the diet still followed today in monasteries, temples, and retreat centers—modern-day sanctuaries to heal us both from within and without. Many participants of weekend retreats at Tassajara, the successful Buddhist monastery in California, say that the regeneration that they feel at soul level is as much due to the food served at mealtimes as the spiritual exercises they undertake. Tassajara offers a simple but rich vegetarian cuisine of organic produce; a variety of vegetables, grains, and legumes form the basis of every meal. This formula proved to be so successful that the monastery opened what is now a thriving restaurant in San Francisco, where people can have a taste of California-style Buddhist fare anytime.

Zen Food

Handle even a single leaf of a green in such a way that it man-
ifests the body of the Buddha. This in turn allows the Buddha
to manifest through the leaf. This is a power which you cannot
grasp with your rational mind. It operates freely, according to the
situation, in a most natural way. At the same time, this power
functions in our lives to clarify and settle activities and is ben-
eficial to all living things.

—Zen master Eihei Dogen Zenji (1200–1253), *From the Zen*
Kitchen to Enlightenment

The beauty of the Zen monasteries that dot the Japanese rural landscape is as much due to the natural forests and bamboo groves that guard
their privacy as to the quality of meditation that pervades their every corner. Perfectly tended gardens, gravel raked in undulating formations adorn-
ing the passageways, black meditation cushions carefully arranged in the
zendo (meditation hall), where the sound of raindrops upon the garden
rocks deepens the experience of zazen (sitting silently in the lotus position)—the outside has been modeled to mirror the inner enlightenment
cultivated daily by Zen monks and nuns.

One of the most essential functions in a Zen monastery is that of chief
cook, or tenzo in Japanese. From ancient times, this work has been carried
out by teachers well-versed in the Buddha's Way and who have aroused the
bodhisattva spirit (the ability to bring enlightenment upon others) within
themselves. The duty of the tenzo is to prepare the community's meals and
to care for the physical and spiritual well-being of its members so as to
"…enable everyone to practice with their bodies and minds with the least
hindrance." This is how Zen master Zenji explained it in *From the Zen
Kitchen to Enlightenment*, which is still regarded today as a unique guide to
how we can cook in a spiritual, wholesome, and enlightened way. He wrote
the treatise because he was saddened that, although the Buddha's Way had
been followed in Japan for several hundred years, no one had ever written

about the preparation and serving of meals as an expression of buddha-dharma (Buddha's Law).

It is the tenzo's ability to see the soul in food and to cook soulfully for his fellow travelers that makes his office so important to the whole community. This regard can be a lesson for our own households: Let us remember to thank and honor our own tenzos for taking care of us. We don't think twice about thanking a restaurant chef, and yet at home, simple negligence makes many cooks feel that their efforts are forever being taken for granted.

Zen is the practice of awareness in everything in every moment; although zazen is a fundamental application of the Zen Way, meditation is brought to many other activities: gardening, cooking, eating, walking, cleaning, and being. This attitude underscores a spiritual urgency. "Wake up now!" is the inherent message in everything Zen. Eating thus becomes an exercise in enlightenment, and Zen monasteries have their own unique table manners.

The period before the meals is always dedicated to meditation and the silence is carried on to the table, where speaking is forbidden. This may remind us of those horrible silences imposed upon the family by thundering fathers and grandfathers who professed that "not talking at the table is a sign of good manners!" Eating silently, however, can be a very soulful experience. Many of us are forced into eating alone at the office when there are just not enough hours in the day to complete all of our tasks and going out to a restaurant becomes a time-consuming luxury that cannot be afforded. In these moments, we not only save time but we can also practice eating Zen-style.

Zen monks and nuns silently recite sutras before and after each meal. This is the equivalent of the prayer before the meal, as practiced in Christian households. Prayers and recitation of sutras are intended as an honoring of the soul of food and awaken awareness of what we are about to do. They also bring us a few moments of silence and quiet contemplation; disengaging from the activities of the day, we pause before taking nourishment into our bodies.

These are some popular Zen mealtime sutras.

- Considering the meal's effect, we reflect on whence it came.
- Weighing our virtues, we accept this offering.

- To defend against our delusive minds and separate ourselves from our faults, we must first of all overcome greed.
- To cure our bodily weaknesses, we take this fine medicine.
- To attain enlightenment, we now eat this food.

We too often give little thought to the elements that bring food to our table: sunshine, rain, fertile soil, and the people who pick and package it for us. The first sutra draws our attention to where the food came from—this is necessary in order for us to fully appreciate its goodness. All food is an offering of the Earth, and we, as its children, partake in its bounty.

The second sutra reminds us that the Earth goes on producing our food no matter what injury we inflict upon its lands, seas, trees, and animals. The planet is far kinder to us than we are proving to be to it.

Greed, the subject of the third sutra, is that which prevents us from sharing food equally. The Third World's hand-to-mouth is the Westerner's abundance and, although this may seem a painful and unpleasant reminder, this imbalance will not be corrected until it is fully realized by each one of us individually and collectively.

The fourth sutra teaches us that in order to maintain excellent physical health we need to treat food as medicine. We have largely forgotten the healing properties of meals, but this instinct can be reawakened as we pay closer attention to the way our bodies respond to the food that we eat.

The last sutra is an encouragement to attain enlightenment even in the simple act of eating: when we align mind, body, and spirit and focus totally on the action in the moment, we are in satori (Zen enlightenment). Master Shunryu Suzuki Roshi ends his book *Zen Mind, Beginner's Mind* with the sentence "In Japan in the spring we eat cucumbers"—this is it, he is saying: Spiritual wholeness does not need to be grand and otherworldly; it is the very simple act of being here, on a spring day, eating cucumbers.

Zen meals are based on the primitive staples of grains, vegetables, and legumes, forming a delicious and nutritious vegetarian diet. In fact, most temples and monasteries follow this same diet the world over: Throughout the Buddhist countries of Southeast Asia, in Taoist China, and even in some Roman Catholic monasteries, eating mostly vegetarian fare is standard practice. Zen monasteries include in their meals all seasonal vegetables as well as herbs that grow in the surrounding fields, forests, and riverbanks, such as some mountain grass and tree leaves, horsetail, starwort, dandelion, sorrel, wild butterbur, sprouts, wisteria buds, parsley, trefoil, red beans, gingko nuts, and lily bulbs. These ingredients are combined with whole rice and various beans to form a meal that is high in nutrients, proteins, and vitamins.

The monastic diet coupled with meditation has been demonstrated to be the winning formula for the most advanced stress-reduction techniques used in the West today. Applying ancient methods to modern-day malaises such as chronic stress, mental fatigue, and heart disease is proving not only one of the most valid preventative methods but also a system to which patients are responding positively in terms of both health improvements and personal fulfillment.

Meditation and Diet

Simply meditate every day before you take food. Close your eyes and just feel what your body needs. You have not seen any food; you are simply feeling your own being, what your body needs, what you feel like, what you hanker for. This [is] "humming food"—food that hums to you. Go and eat as much of it as you want, but stick to it. The other food [is called] "beckoning food": When it becomes available, you become interested in it. Then it is a mind thing and it is not your need. If you listen to your humming food, you can eat as much as you want and you will never suffer, because it will satisfy you. The body simply desires that which it needs; it never desires anything else. That will be satisfactory, and once there is satisfaction, one never eats more. The problem arises only if you are eating foods which are beckoning foods: You see them available and you become interested and you eat. They cannot satisfy you because there is no need in the body for them. When they don't satisfy you, you feel unsat-

Eating Alone

CLOSE THE DOOR of your office or choose a space where you can
be alone. If your computer is on, turn it off. Put your phone on "call
forward." Relax for two or three minutes by paying attention to the
in and out of your breathing. You may feel like keeping your eyes
closed to disengage from the computer screens or activities of the
mind. Now, unwrap your food and lay it out aesthetically before
you; everything must be there—drink, napkin, cutlery—so that you
don't have to interrupt yourself. Eat slowly, chew carefully, savor the
ingredients that make up your meal and savor them. Swallow each
mouthful before taking another bite. Be total in eating alone: don't
look at documents, magazines, newspapers, or books. Pay attention
to your food. This silence will make you graceful and elegant. Drink
slowly and only after having swallowed each bite of food. Slow your
breathing pattern and allow satisfaction to expand the experience.
Pause when switching from one course to the next; allow your
body to adjust to different textures and flavors. When you finish,
close your eyes, pay attention to your breathing, and be grateful for
the abundance you have received.

isfied. Feeling unsatisfied, you eat more; it is not going to satis-
fy you because there is no need in the body in the first place.

—Osho, *From Medication to Meditation*

The great contemporary master Osho tells us about an ancient yogi
saying that states that the best food is the one that "hums" to you; ordinary food, by contrast, does not emit a low resonance—we are still visually or mentally attracted to it, but when ingested, it may feel like the
wrong kind of meal. Chicken soup is the cliché feel-good food for Jews;
it "hums" and makes them feel spiritually better after eating it. In India,
the land that gave rise to meditation, ancient masters used to teach their
disciples that the first temple is the body. We should worship the body, pay

attention, and care for it so that the soul within us can shine outward. Food is the most basic substance for our health, as it heals us, strengthens us, and ensures our health.

The type and quality of the food we eat and how it is consumed is determined by the degree of awareness of our bodies—the more sensitive, the more perceptive we are, the greater the attention for what we eat. Normally, however, unless we are suffering from a weight or general health disorder, we tend to consume food that we relish—we are attracted to it visually and become hungry for it because of the anticipated pleasure it will give us on our palates. But do we know whether or not it is good for us? Do we know whether it will cause stress or relieve it; whether it will increase our energy or slow us down? Most probably not.

The neglect of our diets affects us immediately and seriously: We may be overweight or underweight, we may be obsessive about food, or we may seriously suffer from lack of energy or be afflicted by a yo-yo dynamism that roller-coasters us from peaks to valleys within a 12-hour cycle. Our temptation is not to relate the activities that go on in our bodies and minds with the kind of food we eat. But if we consider that the only and basic reason that we eat at all is to keep us fueled, then the connection becomes crystal clear. We wouldn't dream of injecting low-quality fuel into our cars, so why would we not pay attention to what kind of food we eat? Some of us may be shocked to discover that we know the mechanisms of our cars better than the inner workings of our bodies.

The role of diets in health and health disorders has been studied for years, and we now know that diet affects our health very quickly. For instance, even a single meal high in fat and cholesterol may induce the body to release a hormone called thromboxane, which causes the arteries to constrict and the blood to clot faster. That is why heart patients get chest pains after eating fatty meals and why so many of them end up in the emergency ward after rich Christmas or Thanksgiving feasts.

We also know that the role of moderate but regular physical activity is vital in maintaining a healthy metabolism—exercise is the second component of the health equation. Studies over the last two decades have proven that stress is the third crucial element for our health. There are two kinds: acute and chronic. We are designed to cope with acute stress far better than with chronic stress, and yet if we stop and examine our modern existence, we would have to admit that most of us meet stress on a daily, if not hourly, basis, and thus are frighteningly familiar with the term "chronic stress" as being a constant in our lives.

Recent pioneering and revolutionary studies by, among others, Dean Ornish, M.D., president and director of the Preventive Medicine Research Institute in Sausalito, California, and by Jon Kabat-Zinn, Ph.D., founder and director of the Stress Reduction Clinic at the University of Massachusetts Medical Center in Worcestor, have scientifically proven that meditation and diet are both extremely important factors in our health. Their studies have provided the missing link in the chain of causes and effects that keep us healthy—meditation addresses our spiritual well-being. The immediate effect of meditation is to make us more conscious of the way we are and thus help us change all those patterns that are harmful to us. Diet and exercise make our bodies fit and sound, stress reduction keeps our minds alert, and meditation awakens our spirits to the beauty and wonder of each moment. Meditation is now considered equal in importance to the other three factors in maintaining our well-being, and no modern health care program is considered complete unless it includes elements of meditation.

Meditation is the art of paying attention, of creating a state in which we are simply silent yet fully alert and, in its deepest state, meditation is the absence of thoughts and the full presence of awareness. This is an ongoing process, an awakened alertness to every action: when we breathe, how we breathe; when we walk, how we walk; when we eat, how we eat. When one is paying attention, there is a subtle but powerful shift of perception. Suddenly, we watch ourselves as though from a distance, and we become less gripped by exterior stimuli—without, however, losing any concentration on our daily tasks. When this shift occurs, we cannot help but be more conscious of how we do things; our concentration increases because we are able to focus more fully upon each moment. The natural consequence of meditation is that we start to care for our bodies, our selves, and others, too. Rather than withdrawing from the world, meditation can help us enjoy it more fully, more effectively, and more peacefully. It brings an increased appreciation to how we feel—we become progressively more sensitive to what is good for us and thus more discerning about how we conduct our lives. The Buddhists call this increased perception *mindfulness* and consider it to be the heart of Buddhist teaching.

Modern medical research and ancient temple techniques are now being combined to re-educate our instincts about how we lead our lives. Many patients who were suffering from severe heart conditions have been healed by adopting a grain-based vegetarian diet—the primitive diet—with meditation. Correct eating is fundamental to our health not only when we are sick but also if we are intent on keeping our well-being and vitality and wish to lead longer, happier lives.

Our natural instinct for food is as a silent, slow, and almost secluded act, very far from the noisy activities of a busy lunchtime restaurant or the quick grabbing of a sandwich from a street corner vendor. Seeing a small baby suckling from her mother's breast is an awe-inspiring experience. Both mother and baby are silent and we naturally feel a reverence for this act. We feel like intruders who should not watch, for it is something private and bond-forming between the two of them.

Dinners with our families and friends can sometimes feel like a blessing and a celebration to our souls—it is not just mere consumption of food but an honoring of life at a deep level. In the past, families used to sit around the table and pray before starting their meals. Prayers before food are a common expression of devotion in many religions. People not only thank their gods for the food served but also stop for a moment of silence, breaking away in their thoughts from daily activities and reaching a different level of awareness before eating. Throughout the East, it is considered unclean to eat unless one has washed. On arriving home in the evening, for instance, all Japanese people take baths before the meal, soaking in clean water, resting and soothing tired limbs, joints, and brains. After bathing, they wear yukatas, simple cotton house robes. Clean, warm, comfortable, refreshed, and relaxed, they can now begin the evening meal.

There is rice in my bag

For ten days,

And a bundle of firewood

By the hearth.

—Ryokan

Modern life has divorced us completely from our natural instincts about food. When we buy it in supermarkets, for instance, we are bombarded by so many stimuli that appeal to the outer senses that our inner sense is completely drowned. By contrast, we all remember the great pleasure and satisfaction of spring and summer days spent planting and picking vegetables and fruits from our gardens, or the pride we feel when we bring back some special food from a country outing: freshly picked strawberries from the field, homemade wine, or natural raw honey.

These items possess greater value than their supermarket equivalents because we know that there are human hands behind their making and packaging. Someone has been in the field to pick fruit for us; someone else has dressed up in a beekeeper's suit to gather the honey. We know of someone who even takes his bees on holidays, packing them on the back of an old van so that they may enjoy different flowers in different fields and thus produce a greater variety of honey. These are people who care about the product, and that care is transmitted to us. They have paid attention and may even have been in a state of silent meditation as they did their work—what they do, and how they do it, is the goodness we buy.

Meditation is not just merely sitting silently in the lotus pose; meditation is about care, appreciation, the heart and soul of life, and everything we are and do in it.

Chapter 2

THE DIET FOR
A NEW HUMANITY

*When washing the rice, remove any sand you find. In doing so,
do not lose even one grain of rice. When you look at the rice, see
the sand at the same time; when you look at the sand, see also
the rice. Examine both carefully. Then, a meal containing the six
flavors and the three qualities will come together naturally.*

—Zen master Eihei Dogen Zenji (1200–1235), *From the Zen
Kitchen to Enlightenment*

Zen Master Eihei Dogen Zenji uses "rice" and "sand" both
literally and metaphorically. Rice represents enlightenment and sand repre-

sents illusion, the two polarities of the spiritual path. All life flows between two opposite poles: dark and light, heaven and Earth, male and female, hot and cold, good and bad, matter and spirit. Everything in nature we can think of contains elements of both. This principle is found in the Chinese theory of yin and yang: All objects and phenomena in the universe can be seen as limitless pairs of opposites.

The yin-yang symbol shows a circle formed by two fish—one white and one black. The white fish has a dark eye and the black fish has a white eye, thus creating a completely balanced picture. The yin principle is everything shadowy, cool, dark, and feminine; it is believed that this power commences in the autumn, overcoming the sun and giving way to the coldness and darkness of winter. The yang principle is the opposite, representing everything that is hot, light, and expansive. Yang power commences in the spring, waking the world from the sleep of winter and making nature grow its bounty through the summer. We have naturally applied this ancient Chinese principle to our own lives and diets: In cold climates (yin), we eat warm foods (yang) and vice versa. When we feel hot (yang), we consume more fluids (yin). When we are greatly active (yang), we need periods of rest (yin). Respecting the law of polar opposites brings us balance, health, well-being, and joy.

The yin-yang principle gives us a very easy method for balancing our diets according to our individual needs. All foods, both solids and liquids, can be divided into essentially yin or yang. In order to maintain health, we need a combination of both. Our immediate environment also contains elements of yin and yang: A stressful, aggressive office is overly yang; our favorite armchair at home, placed in a peaceful, secluded room, is yin. Activities follow the same principle, with working weekdays being yang and relaxed weekends spent with family and friends being yin.

Once we become accustomed to viewing these qualities within ourselves, in what we do, and in the world that surrounds us, we can easily monitor our diets to obtain the maximum potential and benefits. If we are stressed at work, we will eat yin food to ease the tension and obtain clarity and focus. If we are suffering from a winter cold, with fevers and shivers, we will be naturally drawn to yang food to replenish our physical energy and to keep us warm.

Our own internal harmony depends upon the balancing of yin and yang: When we have equal amounts of both in our bodies, we experience harmony as good health and well-being. Start experimenting with the yin-yang correspondences between the foods you eat and the way that you are feeling at any one point in time. Learn by paying attention to your body, mind, and soul.

Food can either increase or decrease our daily stress levels. Below, we give you a learn-at-a-glance guide to the stress levels caused by certain foods. We suggest that you also keep a copy of this handy at home and work. You may want to refer to it when going out to a restaurant at lunchtime, when ordering takeout, or when you're so stressed that you'd do anything to get some peace and quiet!

Foods That Increase Stress Levels	Foods That Decrease Stress Levels
Eggs	Tofu
Meat	Tempeh
Fried food	Pinto, lima, and soy beans
Cheese	Oatmeal
Salmon	Soy products
Cream	Goat's milk
Whole Milk	Tahini
Butter	Unrefined oils
Mayonnaise	Sesame, sunflower, and pumpkin seeds
Nuts	Corn tortillas
Palm and coconut oils	Granola muesli
Avocado	Pies with low-oil crust
Fried chips	Rice Dream
Cookies and cakes of all types	Salads
Pizza	Fresh yogurt

You can prepare some of these items ahead of time and keep them at the home and the office. For instance, tahini sprinkled with toasted sunflower seeds makes a wonderful topping on rice cakes when you get a craving. Try to observe the moments when you feel like grabbing for food because you are feeling stressed; invariably you will feel like eating something sweet. Sugar gives you a temporary high, followed by a low, which you may adjust with yet more sugar. Let craving-watching be your office meditation and find healthier alternatives. Keep instant miso soup packets and corn tortillas with a delicious dip by your desk for one day, and notice the difference when you eat these things rather than sugar—you will eat less and be more satisfied.

Applying the yin-yang principle is not a matter of learning something entirely new. This ancient wisdom recalls our own instinct about what is right for us at any one point in time. Paying attention, being sensitive to how we feel and what we need, approaching life in a meditative way, seeking balance and harmony in our emotions, actions, and relationships—these are the tools that we all possess and that enable us to apply wisdom and enlightenment to our lives. Rather than absorbing yet another dietary system, the yin-yang principle awakens our natural instinct about correct eating; we will choose "humming" food, substances we need rather than crave.

The Modern Diet

Let him extend unboundedly
His heart to every living thing.
—Buddha

Today, we benefit from an abundance of knowledge, technology, and skills in growing the highest quality food, yet suffer from diverse dietary ailments. But in 1988, for the first time in United States history, the Surgeon General acknowledged that two-thirds of all deaths are directly affected by improper diets. Poor eating habits play a large part in the nation's most common killers—coronary heart disease, stroke, atherosclerosis, diabetes, and some cancers. What we need now is an intelligent diet—we need to function at the peak of our energies and to maintain that balance with a minimum of upkeep. Food can act as foundation medicine. If diet is used correctly, we will be less prone to life-damaging illnesses and require less medicine.

This era will in the future be known as the time when convergence between Eastern and Western thinking was most powerful. This fundamental meeting is mirrored in the way we eat as much as it is in many other areas of life. Our supermarkets now stock exotic fruits and vegetables as well as sea vegetables, whole-grain breads and pastas, and staples from Indian, Japanese, and Chinese culinary traditions. Seeing the different produce on the shelves is an open invitation to customers to experiment with other methods of cooking and eating.

Television cooking shows teach us how to prepare meals that originated in faraway parts of the world. These are everyday manifestations of an integration of Chinese food medicine and Occidental nutrition. Thousands of years ago, master healers in the Orient devised simple yet incredibly effective methods of healing their patients with food. Analyzing the human being as a total composite of mind, body, and soul, they created a fully comprehensive spectrum of guidelines about diet as the first and foremost cure for all common ailments.

Asian or Chinese medicine offers a different dimension of food from our own. It recognizes the warming and cooling values of certain ingredients and their ability to moisten, strengthen energy, calm the mind, reduce watery or mucoid accumulations, and counter many other imbalances of the mind, the body, and the spirit. Western nutrition can benefit enormously from the ancient wisdom of the East—while we speak of carbohydrates, proteins, and fats, we can also learn from cleansing, de-stressing, and enlightening foods. The modern diet is the perfect marriage of these two great traditions and the recipes in this book are based upon the most recent discoveries of both areas.

As the affluent West becomes progressively more interested in a holistic approach to the body and to life, we begin incorporating ancient Asian wisdom more and more into our homes. We may combine exercise with meditation and a rich, joyful diet consisting of those nutrient qualities that enhance our health. This is a sign that we are paying attention, bringing ancient temple techniques into our offices and homes, and caring not only about our bodies but also our souls. We are now aware of soul quality in our lives more than in the recent past, and we are making efforts to increase its presence in everything.

The best foods to use for long-term balance of mind, body, and spirit are not extreme; they are mild and centering and form an axis around which other, more extreme ingredients can revolve. These mild ingredients are the complex carbohydrates found in the original diets the world over and are the staples of the primitive diet. This large group contains grains, vegetables, sea vegetables, legumes, nuts and seeds, and fruits—now popularly recognized under the modern term *fiber*.

Complex carbohydrates contain the most balanced amounts of yin and yang energy. They increase, build, and maintain harmony both within our bodies and between us and the environment. The recipes in this book revolve around the intelligent use of complex carbohydrates for maximum health and nutrition. Readers will find that the meals are delicious and easily digested and that they produce large amounts of energy, which allows us to work at our peak efficiency without snacking between meals.

Complex carbohydrates also accomplish another, perhaps more magical function: When our diets are based on them, we feel more peaceful, more alert, and naturally more soulful. This is because we have drastically reduced our intake of toxic substances, which cause havoc in our digestive systems and keep vital organs, such as the liver, working overtime to reestablish the balance lost by our way of eating. When our bodies are nourished with a healthy, clean diet, something happens to the rest of us—our energy channels clear, our abilities to focus increase, our weight returns to normal levels, we are less prone to sickness, and, unburdened by poisons and toxins, we feel happier and naturally closer in spirit to the rest of life.

A Vegetarian Diet

The modern diet is ultimately a vegetarian one based upon the extensive and expert use of complex carbohydrates. The recipes in this book follow a vegetarian way of nutrition and have been carefully devised for maximum vitality and variety in their presentations. Food for the spirit does not require the taking of animal life, but it demands that we recognize soul quality not only in ourselves, our homes, and our relationships but also in the world that surrounds us, in the animals and plants.

We very seldom see the way domestic animals are bred, fed, and killed before they reach our tables. Images of this process deeply affect our human sensitivity. The debate over the British problem of bovine spongiform encephalopathy (mad-cow disease) alerted a large proportion of the public to the fact that the quality of animal life and health is often sacrificed in order to satisfy our demand for beef. As soon as news images of diseased cows, of the contents of their feed (protein derived from, among other things, sheep's entrails), and of their inevitable destiny at the slaughterhouse reached our homes, many of us felt that this was a very cruel and unnatural way of treating farm animals.

Shopping in supermarkets, although very convenient, ultimately robs us of the direct experience of the origins of food. If we really knew and saw the ingredients of canned food, the farms where the animals are kept, or the fields where our grains are harvested, we would have an entirely different approach to shopping. Even the act of thinking about these issues already changes our perception of nutrition. When we begin to think in terms of energy forces—the energy of something outside being introduced into our own interior—then our sensitivity to food and the way we prepare our meals increases a thousandfold.

Many people are under the impression that the absence of meat in the diet leads to a grave protein deficiency. However, when certain vegetables, legumes, and grains are combined intelligently, they offer better quality protein than meats. Toxins in plants and grains are far fewer than in meats and are readily neutralized in the process of cooking. In order to be preserved, meat needs to be treated with nitrate (a toxic substance for us), which is released at different cooking temperatures. When meat toxins are introduced into the acidic climate of our stomach, they create serious internal disarray—so our stomachs need to work harder to digest meat.

The recipes in this book also make minimal use of dairy foods and eggs, two of the most prevalent allergens today. We are so used to including these ingredients in our meals that we have no experience of what would happen to our bodies if we were to eliminate them for a while or dramatically decrease their use in our daily food. The meals are an invitation to try and see what happens; those suffering from skin or respiratory allergies will notice a remarkable difference in a very short time. Those not affected by allergies will also recognize the benefits of a dairy-free diet: Their weight will drop and they will generally feel less obstructed and more energetic.

Vegetarianism does not lead to enlightenment. Jesus ate meat and completely transformed centuries of spiritual thinking, and so did many others like him. The increased awareness, however, that comes from meditation, from caring for ourselves and others, does dramatically alter the way we feel about the world. Meditation renews the bond between the individual and the universe that surrounds us, and this includes the animal kingdom. It is very difficult to dig your knife and fork into a carcass that has been fried and call it a good meal when you are in a state of increased sensitivity and perception. Meditation also alters our appreciation of aesthetics—spirituality goes hand in hand with beauty. When this is applied to our diets, it is simple to see how the sense of aesthetics can be enhanced far more with vegetables and grains than with dead animals.

In Asian countries, rich in their traditions of spirituality and meditation, even the ordinary householder follows rules of asceticism. The whole of Hindu society, for instance, cultivates the ideal of ahimsa, or noninjury. This is the absence of the desire to harm, manifested in the Hindu preference for a vegetarian diet and in the worship of the cow, an animal which gives food without needing to be killed. In the East, most people know that eating pure food leads to a purity in the physical, mental, and spiritual ecosystem.

Organic Food

The Earth does not belong to us. We belong to the Earth.
—Chief Seattle of the Suqwamish and Duwamish, an ally of the
White man and a key figure in the agreement to settle the
Washington tribes in reservations in 1855

The vitality gained with food for the spirit is also based upon the attention and respect we give to the preparation of our meals. When we care about how we are chopping, slicing, boiling, and finally, laying out the ingredients that we have prepared on serving dishes, the quality of the meal is enhanced. Our attention creates a certain atmosphere around the table and this can be applied not only to our family dinners but also on those occasions when we invite friends. The success of dinner parties is in the combination of the right people—the right atmosphere is created by the hosts and the guests feel cared for and happy. The more we pay heed to atmosphere and to the quality of certain moments, the more these are revealed to us. It is like looking into a wishing well and seeing all of the patterns and shapes;

the more we look, the more we can read the secrets and revelations in the water.

Finding spirit in food also leads us to greater awareness of what kind of food we buy. Most cities and small towns have a few stores or supermarkets that specialize in organic food or have a section dedicated to organic produce. In its original sense all food is organic because it comes from plants or animals. In the last 50 years or so, however, the term "organic" has been used to describe food grown without fertilizers or pesticides and in a way that emphasizes crop rotation, so as to ensure that the life of the soil has been maintained.

Organic fruits and vegetables have been grown in a traditional, environmentally friendly way. Organic farmers follow organic production systems, which are designed to produce optimum quantities of food of high nutritional quality, by using management practices that minimize damage to the environment and wildlife. These include working with natural systems rather than seeking to dominate them; the encouragement of biological cycles involving microorganisms, soil flora and fauna, plants, and animals; the maintenance of valuable existing landscape features and adequate habitats for the reproduction of wildlife, with particular regard to endangered species; careful attention to animal welfare; the avoidance of pollution; and consideration for the wider social and ecological impact of the farming system.

A great deal of care, soul, and attention goes into organic farming, and as a consequence, the products are more expensive than the average fruits and vegetables that may have been sprayed with harmful pesticides and grown with chemical fertilizers. The trend, however, is that the public is increasingly demanding that such products be sold in ordinary supermarkets and that an extensive range of health foods be offered on their counters. The more we care about the soul, the more discerning we become about the environment and how to treat it. In the future, we will see a greater abundance of organic produce selling in our supermarkets at affordable prices. And organic fruits and vegetables that are in season and grown locally are generally not more expensive than their nonorganically cultivated counterparts. The difference, however, is remarkable: They taste better and are more fulfilling. You will also want to eat comparatively less organic produce, as all the original vitality has been preserved in the fruits and vegetables, making less satisfy more.

Going to the Market

There are few things more beautiful than freshly picked fruits and vegetables and few joys greater than going off in the morning to a farmers' market to purchase them. Most cities today host a market at least once a week, and this is one of the most dependable, most economical sources of fresh ingredients one can find. Here, once a week, year-round, organic farmers offer their produce in simple stalls, making available everything you need for your week's menus. In fact, we suggest that you plan your meals around what you find at the market, as everything offered is at its ripest and freshest.

Going to the market is great fun; everyone is a food-lover there. There are foragers who climb steep hills, returning with baskets full of wonderful mushrooms. There are fruit-growers proud of their orchards; farmers who will discuss endlessly with you the quality of their potatoes, tomatoes, and eggplants; and berry-growers who have specialized in just a few crops. Some stalls sell fertilized eggs laid by hens that roam freely and that are raised on vegetarian diets free of hormones. Others offer a wonderful array of cheeses, while still others offer up freshly baked breads and pastries.

Keep your eyes open while you shop, and let yourself be led by your senses: Which lettuces are humming at you? Those are the ones that you want to buy. Talk to the stall-keepers and you will find that they each have a story to tell. If you patronize farmers' markets every week, you will soon find yourself making friends with the people, and you will acquire a greater knowledge as to how and where your food was grown. This is a great family outing, too, as children love markets and love being involved in the shopping process, helping carry baskets full of edible treasures.

Living in Harmony with the Seasons: The Chinese Five Element Theory

The Five Element theory was developed thousands of years ago by Chinese sages who saw the limitless correspondences between the workings of the human body and the workings of nature. It is a simple and yet effective way of describing the constitution and condition of any individual at any one point in the year. The five elements—wood, fire, earth, metal, and water—correspond to the five seasons—spring, midsummer, late summer,

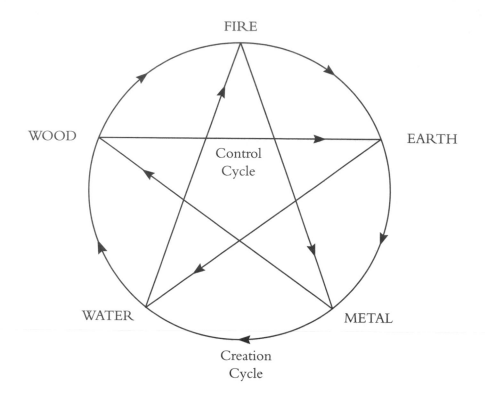

FIRE

WOOD

EARTH

Control
Cycle

WATER

METAL

Creation
Cycle

autumn, and winter. Between these two parameters there exist other sets of correspondences between the insides of our bodies and the environment. Each element and season also relates to a physical organ, to a taste, to a degree of yin-yang balance, and to certain foods that help us attune to the seasons.

The Five Element theory is a workable model that allows us to see all the natural correspondences and how we are affected by them. The elements, and everything that relates to them, influence one another either positively, forming a creative cycle, or negatively, forming a destructive cycle. The creation cycle can briefly be explained as:

Wood burns to make
Fire whose ashes decompose into
Earth where they are born and mined as
Metals which enrich
Water which nourishes trees (Wood)

The destruction cycle is explained as:

Wood is cut by Metal

Fire is extinguished by Water

Earth is penetrated by Wood

Metal is melted by Fire

Water is channeled and contained by Earth

We all know that we need to brace ourselves against a very cold day with layers of warm clothes, hot stews, and stimulating beverages. We might feel, however, that spring is a very disorienting season, taking us through highs and lows of energy, affecting our heads and our general re-energizing potential. Each change of season causes a natural and powerful alteration in our emotions and metabolisms. Spring, for instance, stimulates us to outdoor activities, such as gardening and long walks, during which we inhale large quantities of oxygen; such aerobic exercise helps us get rid of winter fats. Eating light foods in spring is essential to aid the liver function properly. If we ignore these signs, stay mostly indoors, and maintain a winter diet, we may suffer as a consequence from mood swings, irritability, and anger.

The Chinese Five Element theory will show us exactly what we need to do to strengthen the flow of life in those key organs that control our well-being in each season. The accuracy of this ancient method is still a source of wonder to modern nutritionists today. Here, we give readers a working, practical knowledge of the system in conjunction with the recipe section that follows. This is to maintain harmony and is not constructed to be a healing method for illness. If you are interested in finding out the medicinal properties of this system or wish to be cured from sickness, we suggest that you consult a Chinese nutritionist.

Harmony with the seasons should be second nature to balanced people. As summer draws to a close, for example, we are already aware that autumn and winter are just around the corner, and so our bodies and minds make gradual arrangements, day by day. We wear warmer clothes, adjust to progressively less light; we begin to think about indoor activities and adopt a more contemplative mood. Each season has its beauty and magic, and adjusting to the changes around us makes us feel more in tune with nature and the bounty that is brought to us every day.

Season	Organs	Element
Spring	Liver and gallbladder	Wood
Midsummer	Heart and small intestine	Fire
Late summer	Spleen and stomach	Earth
Autumn	Lungs and large intestine	Metal
Winter	Kidney and bladder	Water

The recipes in the following section of this book are organized according to the five seasons—spring, midsummer, late summer, autumn, and winter. They have been carefully worked out in relation to the seasons' availability of fresh produce, and many guidelines are given as to what cooking methods are best to employ in each season. Above is a basic chart to show the correspondences between the seasons, the elements, and the organs of the body, according to the Five Element theory.

Understanding the interconnection between all the elements of the universe that surrounds us enhances our own senses of harmony and unity so we can flow with change rather than react against it. Diet, being that part of the environment with which we directly nourish ourselves, plays a very important part in maintaining this subtle balance. Harmony means good health.

Re-energizing Foods	Stress-Causing Foods
Sour taste: quinoa, barley, lemons, plums, daikon radishes, broccoli, cabbage, celery, carrots, parsley, and sea vegetables	Alcohol, dairy products, eggs, meats, and foods with chemical additives
Bitter taste: Chicory, corn, spring onions, all summer vegetables, and local fruits	Alcohol, dairy products, eggs, meats, and foods with chemical additives
Sweet taste: Pumpkin, parsnips, carrots, sweet vegetables, onions, millet, miso, and kombu sea vegetables	All processsed foods, monosodium glutamate, fats, and fruit juices
Spicy taste: leeks, garlic, ginger, root vegetables, brown rice, hijiki sea vegetables, miso, pears, and apples	White flour, yeast, and fats
Salty taste: beans, buckwheat, sturdy green vegetables, miso, soy sauce, adzuki beans, and berries	Chilled foods, raw foods, and sugars

Making the Transition from a Meat-Eating to a Vegetarian Diet

A successful transition to a vegetarian diet needs to be a gradual process. It may take months or perhaps even years until the body fully adapts to a radical switch of eating habits. If you have been eating meat all your life but would now like to switch to a vegetarian diet, you should seek the help of an expert nutritionist who can discuss your individual needs and biological rhythms so your health is maintained throughout the transition. Following are a few suggestions and tips. Do not rush; allow your body to make the transition at its own pace. (For more information on plant-derived protein sources, see "Health Food Supplements" on page 61.)

- Gradually substitute refined grains with whole grains, such as brown rice, whole-wheat pasta, or unrefined organically grown cereals.
- Gradually replace products that cause loss of minerals and nutrients, such as sugar and alcohol, with natural sweeteners—honey, molasses, maple and rice syrups—and more natural beverages.
- Begin using sea vegetables in your diet as they contain the whole spectrum of minerals.
- Use more vegetables and try to avoid eating red meats. Start planning your meals around the grain, legume, vegetable axis. Progressively reduce all meats, then fish and fowl. At the same time, reduce your intake of dairy foods like eggs and milk.
- Keep your meals nutritious, balanced, and light. Sometimes combining complex carbohydrates such as brown rice with dairy foods can cause blockages in the digestion.

You may find that your eating habits change quite dramatically. Or you may prefer to have small quantities of food often—a bowl of rice, a cup of miso soup—rather than having two large meals a day. Pay attention to the energy flow in your body and mind throughout the day and perhaps draw up a chart. If you feel more hungry in the morning, then have a nutritious breakfast and a substantial lunch, and end the day with a snack for dinner. Discuss these changes with your family and encourage them to chart their natural energy rhythms in a 24-hour cycle. Experiment and be playful; eventually you will find your perfect balance.

Planning Your Meals

Attain the climax of emptiness,
preserve the utmost quiet:
as myriad things act in concert,
I thereby observe the return.
Things flourish,
then each returns to its root.

Return to the root is called stillness:
stillness is called return to Life,
return to Life is called the constant,
knowing the constant is called enlightenment.
—Lao Tzu, *Tao Te Ching*

The best possible diet is a balanced one that addresses all your needs. As you progressively switch from a meat-eating to a vegetarian diet, your hunger patterns will also change. Complex carbohydrates such as brown rice, millet, kasha, and the many other grains suggested in the recipe section provide you with slow-burning energy that sustains you for long periods of time. When you include grains in your daily diet, you will find that you need to eat less at each meal and that you will not feel hungry between meals, with the need to snack slowly falling away. Observe your hunger patterns closely over a period of one to three months.

Maybe you will want to keep a journal in which you can log your progression as your body becomes accustomed to a vegetarian diet. It is a good idea to draw a clock for every day and to highlight the times when you feel hungry in one color and the times when you feel satisfied in another color. In this way you will be able to get an instant visual picture of your natural eating patterns and you will be able to plan your meals accordingly. The clock will also help you see what your low blood sugar–level times are. (For healthy alternatives to get you through the low-sugar blues, see "Snacks and Low Blood Sugar Levels" on page 40.)

Most of us naturally fall within three eating patterns. Some people are satisfied with one big meal a day and don't really feel hungry at all throughout their 24-hour cycle, although they may have a very small snack at some point in that cycle. Other people, however, are happiest with two main meals a day—this represents the majority of adults leading active lives. And the third group feels that unless they eat three meals a day they lack energy, are unmotivated in their work, and easily become cold and tired. Here are some suggestions on how to best plan for these three eating patterns. (To plan your diet properly, you should first consult an expert nutritionist.)

One meal a day: Japanese and American Zen Buddhist monks maintain a single-meal dietary practice for several reasons. First, there is plenty of time for the digestion and assimilation of food, allowing organs such as the small intestine and the liver to complete their functions before the processing of their next meal begins. Secondly, the single meal is generally eaten at noon, a time when intuitions are heightened and the choice of what is eaten and how it's eaten is clearer. Finally, because the experience of meditation is deepened when the body is not in the process of digesting food, less sleep is needed and thus more hours can be dedicated to silence and contemplation.

The quantity of food eaten in the one daily meal should be moderate and not be that of two or three meals. A certain austerity and discipline is needed as you will have to be careful in the planning of this one meal so that you get everything you need from the diet and yet don't overeat. The foods need to have ample variety, placing emphasis on raw or slightly cooked items as well as on grains and dark, leafy green vegetables. Ideally, this meal should be eaten between 11:00 A.M. and 1:00 P.M.

Two meals a day: This is a perfect eating schedule for those who have adjusted well to a grain, legume, and vegetable diet. It's best to wait at least an hour after waking in the morning before having your first meal. You may start by drinking a fresh raw fruit or vegetable juice and wait until you feel really hungry before consuming more substantial food. The best times for the first meal are between 7:00 and 9:00 A.M. as this is when you are likely to feel most hungry and in need of nourishment after the night. This meal should be moist to help with morning dehydration—if you are eating cooked cereals, for instance, add more water while cooking to obtain a soft and moist consistency. You can eat a combination of raw and cooked ingredients, such as fruit salad with porridge or hot cream cereal.

Many people feel that eating a substantial breakfast and drinking plenty of liquids during the day gets them through until supper time, and they don't really feel hungry at noon. Many of us feel that lunch slows us down in the afternoon. We may feel sluggish, bored, unmotivated, and even sleepy. If this is the case, then the digestive process is using up the energy that should go into work. Try the two-meal-per-day schedule for a few days. If you get low blood sugar levels in mid-afternoon, read the following section, where we give some suggestions for healthier alternatives to sweets and coffee.

The second meal should ideally be eaten in mid-afternoon or before sunset and at least two hours before going to sleep. The later the meal is eaten in the day, the smaller it should be so as to allow for good digestion and restful sleep. The second meal should include foods that are soothing and that prepare you for the night, such as soup or some root vegetables and concentrated proteins such as lentils, tofu, or tempeh. Add some dark green, leafy vegetables to your supper.

Three meals a day: This is perhaps the most traditional eating schedule for most people, and if you were raised on three meals a day as a child, then continue on this program until your body signals that it is time for a switch.

The first meal should be eaten between 7:00 and 9:00 A.M., and it should contain plenty of water. Try alternating cooked and raw ingredients on different days. For instance, you can have a bowl of fruit with maple syrup and herbal tea on Monday morning and, on Tuesday, cook rice cream with some raisins and sprinkled with dry coconut flakes. On Wednesday, you can again have a fruit salad, and so on.

The second meal, eaten usually at noon or shortly thereafter, can be the largest meal of the day. This is when you can eat large salads that will keep you cool and clear through the difficult low blood sugar–level afternoons. It is important to have a variety of ingredients both cooked and raw.

The third and last meal of the day, to be eaten between 4:00 and 7:00 P.M., should be the smallest and should contain the most protein; good sources are legumes, seeds, nuts, and dairy products. Cooked root vegetables—potatoes, turnips, parsnips, and carrots—are also best eaten at this time of day to sustain you through the night.

As with any eating plan, most people experience early morning thirst. In fact, we often wake up thirsty but not hungry—and if we drank alcohol the evening before, the thirst will be even greater. It is important that we pay attention to our dehydration levels both during the night and early in the morning. Keep a glass of still mineral water at room temperature by the bedside and drink it in small sips whenever needed. Fluids are required to help the purification process that is occurring as your digestive system is processing the foods of the day. In the morning, you should drink a glass of water with a few drops of lemon juice, or a flower tea such as chamomile, orange blossom, or jasmine—these are highly purifying and will help you in the transition between sleep and the high energy of the day.

Early morning is the most important time for cleansing as this is the time one has been without food longest. If you have been eating and drinking late, this is the time when you can bring a fresh balance to your body again. Start with a glass of water then drink a glass of raw fruit and vegetable juice. Eat raw fruit if you are hungry and thirsty or cooked fruit if you are feeling under the weather and cold. A clean meal early in the morning is the best remedy for any excesses of the night before. It will set you anew and help you regain your energy during the day.

Snacks and Low Blood Sugar Levels

Although the body may respond quickly and positively to a dietary change, it will still take some time for a complete adjustment. When sugar levels fall, we may feel some or all of these symptoms: tiredness, fatigue, restlessness, depression, lack of attention to what we are doing, and general weakness. The normal tendency is to snack on either very sugary snacks, such as chocolate, sweetened yogurt, or biscuits, or very salty ones, like potato chips or other salty packaged snacks, or to drink a cup of coffee.

Following are reasons that we should minimize the intake of these particular foods and suggestions for some alternatives. (For more information about the benefits of some of these products, see chapter 3.)

Sugar: Our culture instills a powerful urge for sweetness from an early age and eating sugary foods is a habit that is sometimes difficult to break. Sugar requires the production of insulin for metabolism, a process that promotes the storage of fat. Metabolized sugar is transformed into fat globules that deposit themselves all over the body where muscles are not very active, like on the chin, stomach, and hips.

Excess sugar upsets mineral balances in the body and that is why it is so detrimental in children's diets. It particularly drains away calcium and dissolves B vitamins in the digestive tract before they have a chance to impart their benefits. Sugar also plays a part in many psychological reactions; it is a food we eat in order to "cope" with stress and tension, as it seems to satisfy holes in our palates and psyches. In reality it produces an over-acidic condition in the body, stripping out stabilizing B vitamins. And satisfaction is exactly what you cannot get from eating sugar. Healthier alternatives are maple syrup, honey, molasses, barley malt, rice syrup, and date sugar.

Salt: Excessive amounts of salt are found today in almost all packaged foods, restaurant dishes, animal foods, and processed and refined foods. Excessive salt causes heart disease, hypertension, and other blood pressure problems; circulation is constricted; kidneys malfunction; fluid is retained; and migraines occur frequently. Too much salt can also produce hyperactivity, aggressive behavior, and poor glandular health. We need to reduce salt intake considerably, but we must not eliminate it completely from our diets; adequate salinity is needed for good intestinal tone, strong blood, tissue transportation of nutrients, and healthy organs and glands. Regular table salt, however, is almost totally devoid of any nutritional value, causing more harm to our metabolism than good. Some healthy alternatives are tamari, soy sauce, miso, umeboshi plums, sea vegetables, sun-dried sea salt, herb salts and seasonings, and sesame salt (also called gomashio).

Coffee: There is good and bad news about caffeine. Moderate use of caffeine has been hailed for centuries for its therapeutic effects. Caffeine is a plant-derived neutroceutical—part of both foods and medications. There is solid evidence for the positive effects of caffeine on mental performance, including clearer thinking and shortened reaction times. In modest doses it improves mood and increases alertness through the release of adrenaline into the bloodstream. It mobilizes fatty acids into the circulatory system, facilitating greater energy production, endurance, and work output.

On the other hand, caffeine in excessive amounts can produce migraines, irritability, stomach and digestive problems, anxiety, and high blood pressure. As an addictive stimulant, it works as a drug, causing nervous jumpiness and heart palpitations as well as heart disease.

The most common reason for drinking excessive amounts of coffee is to combat fatigue, especially at work. We need stimulants to create a sense of well-being, exhilaration, and self-confidence. There are natural energizers that have great advantages over chemically processed stimulants. They have a more broad-based activity, so they don't deplete a particular organ or body system. And they are nutrient supportive, rather than depleting. Try these healthy alternatives to excessive coffee intake: guarana, kola nut, maté tea, ginkgo, royal jelly, ginger, or CoQ_{10}.

Snacking at the office: When we feel a depletion of energy during office hours, we tend to grab either a bag of something salty and greasy or something sweet and gooey. But there are healthier alternatives, such as rice cakes or whole-meal crackers topped with a homemade sauce.

(continued on page 44)

Some Basic Nutrients and Their Availability in Natural Sources

Nutrient	Benefits
Proteins	Constitute 20 pecent of total body weight. Proteins are building blocks for muscles, blood, skin, bones, the brain, and heart. They play a vital role in growth and regeneration.
Carbohydrates	They are a supply of energy and thus must constantly be supplied and replenished. Complex, slow-burning carbohydrates are the only source of fuel for metabolism. In case of deficiency, the body breaks down proteins in order to get its fuel supply.
Vitamins	These are micronutrients that need to be supplied in the diet as they are not part of the body structure. They help regulate chemical reactions within the metabolism. Vitamins that we derive from the diet can be destroyed by smoking, stress, alcohol, and an excessive intake of protein. Nutritional needs of vitamins vary tremendously and change dramatically during crisis, illness, pregnancy, and breastfeeding. If taken in supplement form, these need to be derived from a food source as synthetic vitamins cause toxicity in the body.
Minerals	They play a vital role in the absorption of vitamins, regulate the pH balance of the blood, and maintain the immune system. Minerals are present in the soil and are preserved in organic foods.
Fats	Despite their bad reputation, fats are needed by the body in moderation. They help the absorption of certain vitamins and minerals. They are also essential to cell structure, maintaining supple skin and making hair shine.
Calcium	This is the mineral found in bones and teeth. It regulates heartbeat and skin balance. It is also responsible for good skin and has a soothing effect on the nerves.

Food Sources

Soybeans, watercress, sea vegetables, green peas, bean sprouts, broccoli, Brussels sprouts, cauliflower, kale, mushrooms, and mustard.

Brown rice, barley, buckwheat, rye, bulgur wheat, oatmeal, beans, and seasonal vegetables.

Alfalfa, apricots, carrots, oranges, winter squash, leafy greens, nuts, beans, soy food, kelp, mushrooms, bean sprouts, seeds, and seasonal vegetables.

Opt for the organic or nitrate-free form of the following: raw seeds, nuts, alfalfa, pollen, brewer's yeast, kelp, molasses, black pepper, cloves, and thyme.

Oils extracted from whole foods without refining. Polyunsaturated, unrefined, cold-pressed olive; corn and sesame oils are best.

Sesame seeds and the paste made from them (tahini), soybeans, peanuts, green vegetables, almonds, sunflower seeds, milk, and cheese.

Homemade sauces taste delicious; do not have flavorings, colorings, or preservatives; and are thus a great deal more healthy than the supermarket equivalents. Take some to the office and use them as spreads on rice cakes to combat sugar cravings or to help you through low-energy periods.

The Importance of Raw Foods and Vegetable Juices

Raw foods and fresh vegetable juices must be included in everyone's diet and should be made into a staple of everyday eating habits. They contain a broad array of vitamins, minerals, and enzymes that enhance and complement individual nutrients. As raw foods are not processed, they are assimilated by the body with little effort by the digestive system and have one of the strongest impacts on building our health. By adding raw foods and fresh vegetable juices to a balanced diet, you will improve and accelerate the process of restoring nutrients to chemically starved tissues.

Spring, midsummer, and late summer are obvious seasons for eating a variety of raw foods, but try to include in your diet raw foods, salads, or carrots and celery sticks in all seasons. Fresh juices, made from either vegetables or fruits or a combination of the two, are vitamin bombs. They are absorbed directly into the bloodstream and are easily digested. The minerals in fresh juices are very different from those we take in supplement form because they are naturally chelated (bonded with) vitamins and amino acids and thus are easily absorbed into the bloodstream.

Easy-to-assimilate minerals are essential in the diet as they keep the body's energy level high, the nerves calm, and the muscles, heart, hair, teeth, and bones strong. Buy a juicer for your home and office (or find a good juice bar near where you work), and switch from compulsive coffee drinking to juice drinking. You'll notice an enormous difference in how you feel after the first glass. Minerals help us keep the blood clean and pH levels balanced. Juices literally transfer the vital qualities of plants and fruits directly into our bodies, and they represent the most natural form, apart from water, of purified fluids, which are essential to our health. Drinking fresh juices does not tax our elimination organs—the kidneys and the liver—because the body absorbs all the nutrients directly and does not have to process harmful substances.

Experiment and try your own cocktails and combinations—variety is extremely important in maintaining a healthy and balanced diet—or see "Fruit and Vegetable Juices" on page 110 for some tried-and-true juice recipes. Choose vegetables and fruits that are in season. Organically grown produce is obviously the best and many suppliers sell boxes of washed carrots and other bulk products at a slightly discounted price. Check your local farmers' market about the availability of buying in bulk at a reduced price. If you are buying in supermarkets, choose items that have been grown locally; because you are eating them raw, you want to minimize the amount of pesticides and chemical fertilizers that have been sprayed onto your produce. Also, locally grown produce spends less time on a truck between farm and store—ensuring further nutritional value.

Chapter 3

A PRACTICAL GUIDE
TO HEALTH FOODS
AND SUPPLEMENTS

WHILE IT MAY BE VERY DIFFICULT to strike personal relationships with the staff in a supermarket, one of the great joys of shopping in small stores is that you can have a one-on-one rapport with each person working there. This is especially true in health food stores, which are generally vision-led by employees who have a keen and informed interest in the products they are selling. You can talk to them, ask for advice, exchange tips, and generally cultivate soulful relationships with the people you're buying food from. Start visiting your local health food store, and while you are shopping, ask questions about what you are buying. You should also find out where your nearest organic grocer is and whether weekly home deliveries are offered, as this is a very convenient service. You can buy certain items, such as grains or carrots and apples for juicing, in bulk for long-term storing.

Here is a brief summary and glossary of those items that appear in the recipes. Use it as a guideline, but we encourage you to experiment on your own and get acquainted with the products as you buy and use them.

Grains

Grains play a fundamental part in any vegetarian diet—they are high in complex carbohydrates and low in fat, and small quantities provide great nourishment. Grains are the staple food for the spirit—they connect us to the Earth and enhance receptivity, relaxation, and centeredness. Stock a few of your favorite grains in your pantry for the preparation of everyday meals. You may also want to invest in an electric rice cooker—a very convenient kitchen appliance that keeps a constant temperature and cooks all grains to perfection. The Japanese company Zojirushi makes excellent rice cookers in different sizes, which are available from the bigger department stores in both Britain and the United States.

Amaranth: This is a relatively new discovery in the family of grains, even though amaranth is of very ancient origin—the Aztecs used it in their diets. A rich source of protein and calcium, amaranth is also excellent for pregnant or nursing mothers as well as infants. It is best used in combination with other grains, such as wheat, to make it more palatable.

Benefits: The lungs. It is also high in protein, fiber, amino acids, and vitamin C and contains more calcium than milk.

Cooking method: For each 1 cup grain add 2½ to 3 cups water (increasing water improves the tenderness of the cooked grain). Bring to a boil and simmer, covered, for 20 to 25 minutes.

Suggested uses: Sweet cereals, biscuits, casseroles, breads, and soups; you can also sprout it and use it in salads.

Barley: This ancient grain has been used throughout the centuries for its nourishing properties. Barley is milled to remove the indigestible hull. There are two varieties: pearl barley and pot (also known as Scotch) barley. Pearl barley has been processed to remove both the germ and the chaff during milling, removing some of the nutritional value. Pot barley is a rich source of fiber, calcium, and iron. Pot barley is often toasted before cooking to reduce its acid-forming qualities.

Benefits: The stomach, spleen, and pancreas.

Cooking method: For each 1 cup grain add 3 to 3½ cups water. Bring to a boil and simmer, covered, for 50 to 55 minutes.

Suggested uses: Breads, cereals, crackers, soups, and stews.

Buckwheat: This grain is widely used in eastern Europe, China, and Japan. It is well-recognized for containing an almost perfect natural balance of amino acids as well as providing calcium and proteins. The buckwheat plant seems to resist many diseases and can grow naturally without the aid of pesticides. When it is toasted, it is called kasha. This is a grain that produces heartiness and helps the body keep warm, so it is perfect for the chilly days of winter.

Benefits: The intestines (not recommended for people with high blood pressure or flatulence).

Cooking method: Rinse well under cold water, then toast. For each 1 cup grain add 2 cups water. Bring to a boil and simmer, covered, for 15 to 20 minutes.

Suggested uses: Pancakes, stuffings, pastas or noodles, and cereal breads.

Bulgur wheat: This grain belongs to the wheat family and is obtained from boiled, dried, and cracked wheat berries. It is rich in fiber, minerals, and vitamins, providing a wide range of nutritional qualities essential for growth and well-being. It is best used in its organic, unrefined form.

Benefits: The kidneys.

Cooking method: For each 1 cup grain add 2 cups boiling water. Cover and allow grain to stand for 30 minutes (no need to cook it). Fluff it with a fork.

Suggested uses: Pilafs, salads, and stuffings.

Corn: This is a grain that is widely cultivated throughout the world, from Italy and the rest of Europe to Asian countries and North America. It is also a staple of many African diets. Fresh corn contains many vitamins and enzymes and is light enough to eat in the warm seasons. Because of its low niacin content, use corn in combination with wheat germ, peanuts, brewer's yeast, or lime juice.

Benefits: The heart and kidneys.

Cooking methods: To make popcorn, use a dry heat: ⅓ cup corn makes 8 cups popcorn. Use a no-stick pan with a lid. For fresh corn on the cob, boil the ears or roast them.

Suggested uses: Breads, dumplings (gnocchi), polenta, corn tortillas, nachos, and salads.

Millet: A staple grain of India, Egypt, and China, it has also been used throughout the centuries in Europe. In the tale of Hansel and Gretel, little Hansel leaves a trail of millet grains to mark his way home from the depths of the dangerous forest, but the birds eat them and the two siblings get lost and end up in the witch's house.

This is the only grain that causes no acidic reaction in the stomach whatsoever. It is well-known for its antifungal properties and is highly recommended for those who suffer from candida infections. It is very easily digested.

Benefits: The stomach, spleen, and pancreas.

Cooking method: Toast first. For each 1 cup grain add 2½ cups boiling water. Simmer, covered, for 35 to 40 minutes.

Suggested uses: Sweetened cereals, stews, casseroles, stuffings, breads, and pancakes.

Oats: This is the ideal grain for cold weather and is widely used in the everyday diets of cold regions, such as the Scottish Highlands (in porridge) and Switzerland (as the main component of muesli). Oats are a rich source of protein as well as silicon and a variety of minerals, including iron. Whole oats have retained both the bran and the germ, where most nutritional qualities reside. Oats are also immensely helpful in regulating energy swings and in calming the nerves.

Benefits: The spleen, pancreas, and nerves.

Cooking method: Use organic whole oats. For each 1 cup grain add 3 cups water. Soak overnight. Bring to a boil over medium heat and simmer for 45 to 60 minutes. For rolled oats, use 1 cup grain to 1½ cups water. Stir and bring to a boil over medium heat. Cook for 10 minutes. Remove from heat and let it stand for 15 minutes.

Quinoa: Quinoa belongs to the amaranth family and was a staple grain in the diet of the Incas. It is tiny and bead-shaped, similar to couscous. It can be purchased packaged as a grain, ground into flour, or made into pasta. It is rich in protein and calcium, strengthening the whole body. This is an ideal food for those switching from a meat-eating to a vegetarian diet, as it is packed with all the necessary nutrients.

Benefits: The kidneys.

Cooking method: For each 1 cup grain add 2 cups water. Bring to a boil. Reduce the heat and simmer, covered, for 15 minutes.

Suggested uses: Salads, breads, and stuffings.

Rice: This is the staple grain in the modern world, eaten daily throughout Asia. Its ancient origins are found in India, China, and Japan. It has legendary healing powers and has for a long time been associated with Zen Buddhist rituals and traditions. Rice plays a key role in maintaining the flow of life energy throughout the body. Try to eat rice at least three times a week: It is a rich source of B vitamins and has soothing properties for the nervous system. White rice is consumed more widely than brown rice, but the latter retains all its nutrients and goodness, as it is unrefined.

Organic, whole basmati rice is the lightest variety and is recommended for all stagnant conditions, such as water retention. Sweet rice is rich in gluten and high in protein and fat, while sprouted rice is a common herb prescribed by Chinese doctors. Short-grain varieties have a nuttier flavor.

Benefits: The stomach, spleen, and pancreas.

Cooking methods: For long- or short-grain rice, add 1 cup grain to 1½ cups boiling water. Simmer, covered, for 15 to 20 minutes.

For brown basmati rice, add 1 cup grain to 2¼ cups water. Bring to a boil. Simmer, covered, for 35 to 40 minutes. For white basmati rice, add 1 cup grain to 1¾ cups water. Bring to a boil. Simmer, covered, for 20 minutes.

To make sweet rice, add 1 cup grain to 1½ cups water. Bring to a boil. Simmer, covered, for 55 to 60 minutes.

Rye: This is a bitter-flavored grain, highly recommended to reduce conditions of dampness in the body and clear away stagnancy in the liver and gallbladder. It contains considerable levels of fluoride, which is essential for building enamel in teeth. Rye is also a hard grain, suited to harsh, cold climates.

Benefits: The liver, spleen, and gallbladder.

Cooking method: Used mainly in flour form.

Suggested uses: Sourdough breads and biscuits; when sprouted can be used in salads.

Wheat: This is perhaps the most cultivated grain in the Western hemisphere as it is packed with nutrients when used in its unrefined form. It builds yin energy, is beneficial for the heart and mind, and is a rich source of minerals, vitamins, and fiber, promoting growth and health. Wheat berries and bulgur come from the same family. Wheat, however, is known to cause allergic reactions in some people, in which case it is best avoided or substituted with rye or another cereal.

Benefits: The kidneys and nerves.

Cooking method: To make wheat berries, soak the grain overnight. For each 1 cup grain add 3½ cups water. Bring to a boil and simmer, covered, for 1 hour.

Suggested uses: Used mostly in its flour form for breads.

Wild rice: Although used as rice, this is actually the wild seed of an aquatic grass that is now commonly used as a grain. It is closely related to corn and originates from North America. Wild rice provides high-quality protein, vitamins, minerals, and fiber. It is both cooling and diuretic.

Benefits: The kidneys and bladder.

Cooking method: For each 1 cup wild rice add 3½ cups boiling water. Bring to a boil and simmer, covered, for 1 hour.

Suggested uses: Can be used in combination with brown rice, wheat berries, or kasha or in salads.

Legumes

Legumes and beans provide a substantial amount of protein in a vegetarian diet and should be incorporated in at least half of your weekly meals. It is best to use organic legumes, rather than the nonorganic or canned varieties. This, however, means that time will be spent cooking them; most beans take an hour or more to cook. Invest in a pressure cooker, which considerably reduces cooking time (generally by half) without decreasing any of the nutrients.

Stock your pantry with a variety of legumes—they keep for months in sealed glass or plastic jars and can be eaten year-round. The longer you store the beans, the longer they will need to be cooked. Organic legumes tend to be harvested in the same year they are sold; check the dates on the packets and buy them as fresh as possible. Follow the recipes for more elaborate dishes or serve freshly cooked beans in the colorful Mediterranean-style: with a drop of extra-virgin olive oil, a few leaves of basil, some salt, and a topping such as black Greek olives, sun-dried tomatoes, or strips of roasted green and sweet red peppers.

Here are some tips for improving the digestibility of legumes.

- Legumes combine best with greens, nonstarchy vegetables, and sea vegetables.

- Salt or salty seasonings should only be added at the end of the cooking time, so as not to toughen the skins. Salt is needed to aid the digestion of the protein in beans.
- Cook legumes with cumin, fennel seeds, or a little vinegar to avoid forming gaseous reactions.
- Add kombu or kelp to the bottom of the pot to improve digestibility and add flavoring.
- Soak legumes overnight. A little flour helps soften the outer skins. Wash them well and never cook them in the soaking water.
- When boiling, remember to discard the foam that forms on the surface of the water.
- Sprouted legumes contain just as much protein and can be added to salads or stir-fry dishes. Steam sprouts for better digestibility.

Adzuki beans: Originally from Asia, they are now widely available and are one of the most digestible beans. Adzuki beans are best flavored with sea vegetables, soy sauce, scallions, ginger, miso, garlic, and pepper. They combine well with millet and the different varieties of rice.

Benefits: Improve kidney-adrenal function, detoxify the body, and promote weight loss.

Cooking method: Presoak the beans overnight first. Discard the soaking water. For each 1 cup beans add 4 cups water. Bring to a boil and simmer, covered, for 1 hour.

Black beans: Widely used in Latin America and Asia, these sweet beans are a diuretic and build yin energy. They are best combined with rice or corn. Many seasonings go well with black beans, such as onions, fresh chopped tomatoes, green peppers, garlic, lemon juice, and fresh herbs.

Benefits: Warm the body when cold, benefit the kidneys, and act as mild diuretics.

Cooking method: Presoak the beans overnight first. Discard the soaking water. For each 1 cup beans add 4 cups water. Bring to a boil and simmer, covered, for about 1½ hours, or until tender.

Black-eyed peas: Originally a wild species from Africa, they are now common in Western countries. They are a rich source of selenium. Quick to cook and easy to flavor, they are wonderful in salads with sautéed spinach and combine well with many other seasonal vegetables.

Benefits: Reduce toxins from the body and act as mild diuretics.

Cooking method: No presoaking is required. For each 1 cup peas add 4 cups water. Bring to a boil and simmer, covered, for 1 to 1½ hours, or until tender.

Chickpeas: Also known as garbanzo beans, these are perhaps the most popular beans in the Middle East, Asia, Africa, and the Mediterranean countries. Chickpeas are a rich source of iron and unsaturated fat. They're easy to use on their own or combined with vegetables and grains. Cumin, coriander, lemon juice, curry powder, or simply olive oil with parsley are excellent flavorings for dressing these beans.

Benefits: Stimulate the pancreas, stomach, and heart.

Cooking method: Presoak the beans overnight first. Discard the soaking water. For each 1 cup beans add 4 cups water. Bring to a boil and simmer, covered, for 2½ to 3 hours.

Dried peas: There are two varieties—green and yellow—both of which are easy to digest and are mildly diuretic. Good seasonings are onions, bay leaf (remove bay leaf before serving), turmeric, or celery. Dried peas also combine well with many vegetables.

Benefits: The spleen, pancreas, stomach, and digestive process; also act as mild laxatives.

Cooking method: No presoaking is required. For each 1 cup beans add 4 cups water. Bring to a boil over medium heat. Reduce the heat to low and simmer for 1½ to 2 hours.

Fava beans: These sweet-flavored beans have a tough exterior skin that can be removed after soaking. Easily seasoned with onions, fresh chopped tomatoes, herbs, and spices. Used to make stews, salads, and pâtés.

Benefits: The spleen and pancreas; also mildly diuretic.

Cooking method: Presoak the beans overnight first. Discard the soaking water. Remove outer skins before cooking. For each 1 cup beans add 4 cups water. Bring to a boil and simmer, covered, for 1½ hours.

Kidney beans: These belong to a large family of beans that includes pinto, green wax, and mung beans. They are cooling and diuretic but are perhaps the hardest beans to digest, even though they are easy to cook. Chili and hot flavors combine well with these as well as onions, garlic, coriander, and other Eastern spices.

Benefits: Reduces swelling and helps cool body when hot; also mildly diuretic.

Cooking method: Presoak the beans overnight first. Discard the soaking water. For each 1 cup beans add 4 cups water. Bring to a boil and simmer, covered, for 1½ to 2 hours.

Lentils: There are red, yellow, and brown lentils. In European countries, they are a symbol of good luck, and in Germany it's a tradition to eat them on New Year's Eve. They are easy to cook and combine well with many grains and vegetables. Use ginger, onions, bay leaf (remove bay leaf before serving), tomato sauce, or peppers to flavor them.

Benefits: The kidneys, heart, and circulatory system; also mildly diuretic.

Cooking method: No presoaking is required. For each 1 cup lentils add 4 cups water. Cook for 30 to 35 minutes.

Lima beans: Also commonly known as butter beans, these are cooling and nourishing and easy to cook. They go well with herbs such as fresh dill, parsley, and basil and are excellent for making creamy soups.

Benefits: The liver and lungs; they have a high alkaline content and help combat stomach acidity.

Cooking method: Presoak the beans overnight first. Discard the soaking water. For each 1 cup beans add 4 cups water. Bring to a boil and simmer, covered, for 1 to 1½ hours.

Mung beans: These are the king beans of Zen food. Cooling and sweet-flavored, mung beans are well-known for their detoxifying properties, and they increase yin energy. They are also available in a sprouted variety that can be added to salads and stir-fry dishes. Good seasonings are onions, ginger, coriander, chopped tomatoes, and even yogurt.

Benefits: The liver and gallbladder; also reduce swelling and are mildly diuretic.

Cooking method: No presoaking is required. For each 1 cup beans add 4 cups water. Bring to a boil and simmer, covered, for 45 to 60 minutes.

Navy beans: Sweet and cooling, these beans are most commonly prepared as baked beans. Their creamy texture goes well with such seasonings as onions, mustard, or tomato sauce.

Benefits: Skin clarity; also cool the body in warm weather.

Cooking method: Presoak the beans overnight. Discard the soaking water. For each 1 cup beans add 4 cups water. Bring to a boil and simmer, covered, for 1½ to 2 hours.

Pinto beans: They take a long time to cook, but pinto beans hold their shape and are full of flavor. Used in many Mexican dishes, they combine well with onions, peppers, garlic, avocado, and cumin.

Benefits: Contain more calcium and sodium than most beans; also cool the body in hot climates.

Cooking method: Presoak the beans overnight. Discard the soaking water. For each 1 cup beans add 4 cups water. Bring to a boil and simmer, covered, for 2½ to 3 hours.

Soybeans: Cooling and full of nutrients, soybeans are the base component of many soy products, including tempeh, tofu, miso, and soy sauce. They need to be well-cooked in order to be digested are a high source of protein.

Benefits: The arteries, heart, vision, circulatory system, and colon; also eliminate toxins and combat stomach acidity.

Cooking method: Presoak the beans overnight first. Discard the soaking water. For each 1 cup beans add 4 cups water. Bring to a boil and simmer, covered, for 2½ to 3 hours.

Soy Products

The soy products recommended below are essential in a vegetarian diet. They contain easily absorbable protein and many valuable minerals and vitamins. Miso, for instance, is a live food that is rich in the bacterium lactobacillus (the same organism that is present in live yogurt cultures), and is therefore helpful in the digestive process. It also contains 13 to 20 percent protein. Tempeh is a highly nutritious fermented food originally from Indonesia; it contains almost 20 percent protein and is low in saturated fats and rich in the valuable omega-3 fatty acids. The calcium content in tofu can equal that of milk, and tofu also contains minerals such as phosphorus, iron, sodium, and potassium.

When these soy products were made in their original countries—Indonesia, India, and Japan—vitamin B_{12} grew in the bacterial cultures and tiny organisms that generally populate the food in those countries. But now that these products are made in our own sanitized and clean factories, most microorganisms are killed during the process of fermentation; and therefore, the Western-made soy products do not contain a significant amount of B_{12}. For this reason, you should not rely solely on soy products as your source of this important nutrient.

Miso: This is a paste made from fermented soybeans, barley, or rice, and each type has a distinctive color and flavor. The red, dark varieties of miso are fermented longer and are best suited for the cold winter months. The lighter varieties are better for warmer weather. It also contains proteins and amino acids in the same patterns as in meats. Miso should be added to a vegetarian diet at least three or four times a week.

Benefits: Digestion.

Cooking method: Always use unpasteurized miso and add to food during the last minutes of cooking, heating minimally and never boiling, so as not to kill its live bacteria. It is best to keep it stored in a glass jar in the refrigerator for up to two days.

Suggested uses: Add to soups, stews, dressings, dips, and gravies as a salt substitute.

Tempeh: This versatile food is made from soybeans that have been cooked, fermented, mixed with herbs and seasonings, and pounded into strips. It is high in proteins, essential fats, and fiber, so it is a very nutritious food, especially for vegetarians. It can be bought fresh, dried, precooked, or frozen in many health food stores.

Cooking method: Tempeh can be steamed, fried, or broiled.

Suggested uses: Precooked tempeh is excellent in sandwiches. Use tempeh in kabobs, breads, burgers, stuffings, salads, or stir-fry dishes.

Tofu: This is a curd made from processed soybeans that have been soaked, cooked, and blended in various stages. Tofu is a staple product of the Orient, and it is widely used in China, Japan, and Korea. It contains easily digestible proteins, B vitamins, and minerals. It is also low in calories and is very satisfying to the palate. There are three basic types of tofu: silken (very soft), medium, and firm. The most commonly used is firm tofu, which can be bought smoked, deep fried, frozen, or marinated. Though rather bland in its original form, tofu easily absorbs other flavors. Those suffering from dairy-derived allergies can make many creamy desserts and dressings from tofu. Store it in a cool place in an airtight container for up to one week.

Benefits: Relieves stomach inflammation, neutralizes toxins, and cools the body in hot climates.

Suggested uses: Scrambled or served in casseroles, thick sauces, stir-fry dishes, salads, and soups.

Sea Vegetables

Sea vegetables share the common characteristic of being one of the highest sources of vitamins and minerals, containing up to 20 times the minerals of land plants. They are literally wonder foods, providing excellent dietary medicinal value as they detoxify the body, improve liver function, alkalize the blood, and benefit the thyroid. They also have a calming effect on the nervous system when eaten regularly. Widely used in Japanese cuisine, sea vegetables are now sold in health food stores and Asian markets.

Buy a few varieties and incorporate them into your meals at least six times a week. Always rinse sea vegetables thoroughly before using, and soak dry sea vegetables before cooking—longer soaking makes them more tender. Fresh sea vegetables can be sautéed or steamed lightly and served in salads or cooked with tofu or grains.

Agar-agar: This is a gelatin-like sea vegetable that can be bought in either powder or flake form. It is also referred to as kanten or agar.

Cooking methods: Dissolve the powder or soften the flakes by combining 4 tablespoons agar and 4 cups water. Bring to a boil over medium heat, stirring constantly. Simmer for 5 minutes. Stir in the other ingredients of your recipe and pour into molds. Set aside to cool.

To make fruit gels, use fruit juice instead of water and add fruit at the end of simmering. To make vegetable molds, use vegetable broth instead of water and add steamed vegetables and herbs at the end of simmering.

Suggested uses: Gelatins, aspics, and mousses.

Arame: A member of the kelp family, this is a rich source of iodine.

Benefits: Helps control high blood pressure and relieve feminine disorders.

Cooking method: Soak the arame in water for 10 to 15 minutes and let it expand in volume. Drain and chop into 1" pieces. Cook in soups, stews, or grains or sauté or steam lightly until tender and add to salads.

Hijiki: This is a rich source of iron, calcium, and vitamin B_2. Hijiki helps to keep blood sugar at optimum levels and has a calming effect on the nerves.

Suggested uses: It is full of flavor and can be used on its own as part of a main meal. Follow cooking instructions for arame.

Kombu and kelp: These are two marine plants full of the goodness of the sea, both with a very high mineral content.

Benefits: Help the kidneys, thyroid, and with prolonged use help prevent arthritis and rheumatism.

Cooking methods: Cut or break into bite-size pieces. Soak for 20 to 30 minutes in warm water. Discard the soaking water. In a large pot of boiling water, cook the kombu or kelp for 1 to 1½ hours, or until soft. Drain. Roast it until it can easily break into flakes. In a food processor or with a mortar and pestle, grind the flakes into a powder.

Suggested uses: Sprinkle on salads or in soups and stews. When cooked with beans, kombu or kelp can enhance the digestibility of the beans.

Nori: This is the seaweed that is wrapped around Japanese sushi. Known for its high protein content, nori grows as a large flat plant. It can be bought in packets containing paper-thin sheets that are folded into four or in the form of finely ground flakes. It promotes the digestion of fried foods.

Cooking method: The easiest way to prepare nori is to hold it over a flame for about 30 seconds, toasting it slowly until it changes color to a darker shade of green.

Suggested uses: In sushi or cut into tiny strips that can be sprinkled over salads, soups, or grains.

Wakame: In Japan, wakame is used to purify blood. As with other sea vegetables, it is a rich source of calcium and niacin and promotes healthy, beautiful skin and hair.

Cooking method: Presoak the wakame for 3 to 4 minutes. Drain and discard the soaking water. Cut into 1"-thick strips and cut off and discard the tough midrib. In a large pot of boiling water, cook for 45 minutes. Drain.

Suggested uses: In soups and stews and mixed with grains.

Stocking Your Pantry

The following list covers the staples of a healthy pantry. Each of the items is used in the preparation of many recipes and can be found in a well-stocked health food store. Even some larger supermarkets may carry one or two of these products. Many of these products are made and distributed in specific regions by local companies, so brand names may vary widely across the country. The brands suggested below should be found nationwide; also, the staffs in health food stores are often very knowledgeable about the brands and products they offer and should be able to give you more complete details when you are buying your pantry items.

- Amazake: A Japanese sweetener made from sweet rice. It can be used to replace sugar in recipes and can also be used as a refreshing drink. It is available in health food stores in different flavors.

- Arrowroot: This is a starch flour used as a thickening agent. Dissolve the arrowroot in a little water before adding it to the dish you are preparing. (You can find arrowroot in the bulk foods departments of supermarkets, or try the product made by Eden Foods.)

- Bancha tea: Also known as kuki-cha, this tea comes from Japan and is drunk as a healthy, refreshing breakfast beverage. It helps improve digestion. (Try Bancha tea imported by Eden Foods.)

- Barley malt: This is a sweetener made from barley and corn and can be used instead of sugar when preparing desserts. (Westbrae makes an excellent barley malt.)

- Black sesame seeds: These small black seeds can be sprinkled over salads or used in grains for flavoring. They are one of the highest sources of calcium. (They can be bought from the bulk foods departments of supermarkets.)

- Bok choy: This is a leafy Chinese vegetable belonging to the cabbage family. It has thick white stems that turn into dark green leaves. Bok choy is used mainly in summer.

- Daikon: This is a long and quite large radish used extensively in Japanese cuisine. It has a sweet, fresh flavor and its skin can be either black or creamy white in color. It can be bought in Asian supermarkets or in health food stores. Grated daikon aids the digestion of oily foods.

- Dashi: A fish broth made from dried bonito that is available at Asian markets.

- Garam masala: A blend of dry-roasted, ground spices that can be found in Asian markets. Curry powder, which is similar in taste, can be used as a substitute.

- Ginger: This is a pungent root that is widely used as a seasoning in many recipes. Buy fresh, organic ginger to get the best flavor.

- Gomasio: This is a seasoning made from ground sesame seeds and sea salt. It is a very good source of minerals and can be used instead of salt or sprinkled over grains and salads. (Good brands are Maranatha and Eden Foods.)

- Grain coffee: You can choose a decaffeinated variety made from either organic barley or dandelion—these are warming drinks for cold winter mornings and afternoons. (Bamboo or Cafix are two excellent coffee substitutes.)

- Jicama: A tuberous vegetable with brown skin and white flesh. It is crispy and crunchy in taste and can be eaten raw or slightly sautéed. It is very popular in Latin American recipes but can be substituted with water chestnuts if you can't find it at your supermarket.

- Kudzu: A flavorless white starch made from the root of the wild kudzu plant, it is used as a thickener for sauces, soups, and desserts. (Try Eden Foods.)

- Mirin: A sweet, low-alcohol Japanese rice wine that is available in Asian markets and some supermarkets.

- Rice vinegar: This is a very mild vinegar made from fermented rice. It is used mostly in salad dressings. (Eden Foods is one of the best brands.)

- Sencha tea: This is the Japanese green tea favored by Zen monks to promote mental clarity and calmness during meditation. (Try Eden Foods.)

- Shiitake mushrooms: You can buy them either fresh (grown locally) or dried and imported from Japan. They add a strong flavor to stocks and soups.

- Soba noodles: These are Japanese noodles made from buckwheat flour. They can be served either cold as a salad or hot with broth and vegetables. (Try Sobaya or Eden Foods.)

- Tamari: This is an organic soy sauce that is made by fermenting soybeans with sea salt for two years. (Try Westbrae.)

- Udon: These are Japanese whole-wheat noodles and are lighter than soba noodles. (Try Sobaya or Eden Foods.)
- Umeboshi: These are pickled, salted Japanese plums that assist the digestive process by keeping the blood alkaline. Used for their medicinal properties, they are especially good in helping to detoxify the liver. They can be used with cooked vegetables, in salads or salad dressings, or chopped finely and put on corn on the cob. The juice from umeboshi can be added to warm water and drank to relieve hangovers and intestinal disorders. Umeboshi can be found in health food stores and in Japanese supermarkets. (Try Eden Foods or Great Eastern Sun.)
- Wasabi: This is a strong Japanese horseradish paste with a highly pungent flavor. It is used for sushi and in salad dressings. (Try Eden Foods or Great Eastern Sun.)

Health Food Supplements

There are two kinds of nutritional supplements: those derived from food or naturally available substances such as bee pollen or evening primrose oil and those that are man-made to compensate for a lack of vitamins, minerals, or amino acids. If we are healthy and happy, drink fresh raw juices, eat organic produce, follow a wholesome diet, meditate, and exercise regularly, food-derived supplements should be sufficient to help us maintain an optimum degree of health. There may, however, be times and conditions that need more careful examination and additional quantities of essential vitamins, minerals, and amino acids.

Poor dietary patterns that are prolonged over time, chronic stress, hereditary conditions that severely affect the metabolism, chronic illness, extreme depression, pregnancy, and breastfeeding are some of the most common ailments that affect us physically, mentally, and spiritually, causing severe depletions of our resources. If you are experiencing any of these, you should seek the guidance of an expert nutritionist who can help discern which supplements you need. Supplements of any sort should be taken for a minimum period of three weeks and, ideally, up to three months in order to feel the full benefits, and they should be taken in combination with a wholesome diet, meditation, and exercise. Supplements, however, do not replace a healthy diet and lifestyle and should not be used as dietary staples—they help rebalance the system when a deficiency exists but should be decreased as the condition improves.

Following is a list of natural food supplements that can be safely added to your diet in order to maximize health and strengthen your immune system. When buying them, make sure that they are wholly natural and organically grown (prepared without any additives) and that they do not contain gelatin, dairy products, or yeast. Health food stores stock all of these products and will help guide your choices. Take these supplements according to the package directions.

Bee pollen: This is an ideal food supplement for vegans (strict vegetarians who consume no animal, fish, or dairy products) as it is a natural multivitamin/mineral supplement. It contains 35 percent protein, is high in B-complex vitamins, and is a rich source of lecithin, a substance that, among other things, stimulates brain function. Pollen also promotes emotional well-being, prevents colds and flu, has a beneficial effect upon the intestinal tract, and is said to slow down the aging process. It should be taken regularly, up to 30 grams a day, especially in the change of seasons from winter to spring. It is available in powder form, granules, or tablets. (Try bee pollen from a local producer or Y. S. Royal Jelly.)

Brewer's yeast: This is a plant without chlorophyll, which produces the green coloring in plants. It is an excellent source of B-complex vitamins as well as amino acids, protein, iron, and copper. It is known to help maintain appetite, improve digestion, calm the nervous system, and relieve anemia. It is available in powder form, tablets, or flakes. Those suffering from poor digestion benefit from it greatly, although they may experience bloating with large doses. Start on a low dosage and progressively increase your intake over several weeks. (Try Red Star or Kal.)

Chlorella: This is a freshwater alga and a concentrated source of easily digestible protein as well as beta-carotene and nucleic acid, which decreases with age, stress, and pollution. It strengthens the immune system, improves growth patterns, and is extremely beneficial for anemic conditions, chronic constipation, and flatulence. It is available in powder form or tablets. (Try Sun Chlorella or Earthwise.)

Coenzyme Q_{10}: Also called CoQ_{10}, this coenzyme was first discovered in 1957 as a substance present in the body but not manufactured by it, so it needs to be supplemented by diet. Only recently introduced into the market, CoQ_{10} is a catalyst for releasing cell energy, and when its level in the body drops by 25 percent, degenerative conditions are set in motion. Healthy hearts have been found to have high concentrations of the coenzyme. As well as strengthening the heart, it is also a powerful antioxidant. Most people get adequate amounts of it from food, so supplements should only be taken after consultation with a nutritionist. It is available in capsules. (Try Jarrow or Nature's Way.)

Evening primrose oil: This is an edible plant that stimulates the action of the stomach, helps lift depression, and stimulates the spleen and liver. It helps control arthritis and blood pressure and is rich in potassium and magnesium. Evening primrose oil has long been hailed as a good regulator of women's menstrual cycles. It is available in capsules. (Try Health from the Sun or Nature's Life.)

Garlic: This common plant is a natural antibiotic. It dissolves cholesterol in the bloodstream, reduces blood pressure, and helps detoxify the body. It is also a natural source of vitamins and minerals. It is available in capsules. (Try Kyolic or Garlicin.)

Ginkgo: This is perhaps one of the most ancient trees alive on Earth today. It was worshipped by the early Buddhists for its strength and ability to survive for centuries. European studies show that ginkgo increases the flow of blood to the brain, reducing the aging of its tissues. It has been found to have positive effects in treating asthma, memory decline, headaches, and insomnia. It is available in capsules. (Try Nature's Way, Nature's Life, or Rainbow Lite.)

Ginseng: This is the king of herbs, used for centuries in Chinese medicine. It is a stimulant, relieving fatigue and stress. In Chinese medicine it is used as a general tonic for the mind, body, and spirit, and it can act as an antidote to the harmful effects of drugs and chemicals. It also contains vitamins A and E. It is available in tea form, in extracts, and in capsules. (Try Imperial or Gaia Herbs.)

Kelp: This is a sea vegetable and a rich source of minerals. It helps control thyroid activity, regulates the metabolism, strengthens the nervous system, promotes glandular health, and is highly recommended during pregnancy. It is available in tablet form. (Try Nature's Way or World Organic.)

Lecithin: This is a substance in our cells that helps the transportation of fats to different parts of the body and regulates the production of bile, which is critical in fat production and absorption. It is also recommended as a stimulant of brain functions. It is available in granules, capsules, and liquid form. (Try Solgar, Lewis Labs, or Nature's Way.)

Spirulina: This is an ancient food that was used by the Aztecs, although its wonderful properties have only been rediscovered recently. It is a blue-green micro-alga, packed with proteins and minerals that are easily digestible. It has cleansing and detoxifying properties, especially for the liver; provides vitamins A, B_{12}, and E; and is said to have a rejuvenating effect. It also reduces food cravings, especially for animal proteins. It's available in tablet form. (Try Earthwise or Nutrex.)

Wild blue-green alga: This is a water plant that grows wild in the uncontaminated waters of Klamath Lake in the state of Oregon. Native American tribes regarded it to be the sister of the magic peyote and used it for deepening meditation and trance states. Today, it is used to help detoxify the body, aid concentration, and clear away states of depression or melancholy. As its effects on the mind and body are very strong, use it in moderation, starting with a low dosage and progressively increasing to a medium dosage over a period of three weeks. It is available in capsules. (Try Klamath or Solgar.)

Part II

RIGHT
FOOD,
RIGHT
EATING

Chapter 4

THE BASICS

T HE RECIPES BELOW ARE FOR ITEMS you may want to make and keep on a regular basis, as they can be used in other recipes in this book or used as substitutions in your own favorite recipes.

FLAVORED MILKS

These are two standard recipes for delicious flavored milks. You can use any other variety of nuts—cashews, sesame seeds, walnuts—and use the same proportions and procedure. Nuts can also be combined with fruit for a sweeter flavor; try figs, bananas, or apricots. Add cinnamon, honey, or maple syrup, not sugar, as sweeteners. Flavored milks make great spring and summer thirst quenchers. They are also nutritious—and children love them, too. Use them as alternatives to cow's milk or packaged soy milks, for drinking or for pouring over cereal or into tea or coffee. Store them in the refrigerator for up to four days.

Almond Milk

1	cup toasted almonds
1½	tablespoons maple syrup or honey
¼	teaspoon almond extract
2¼	cups water

In a blender or food processor, grind the almonds into a fine paste. Add the syrup or honey, almond extract, and water. Blend for 3 to 4 minutes more. Using a fine sieve or a cheesecloth, strain the milk slowly into a large jug. Use a spoon to gently press the paste and squeeze out the remaining milk. Serve chilled.

Makes about 2 cups

Hazelnut and Date Milk

2¼	cups water
1½	cups toasted hazelnuts
½	cup pitted dates
2	teaspoons vanilla
1	tablespoon maple syrup

In a blender or food processor, combine 1 cup of the water with the hazelnuts, dates, vanilla, and syrup. Blend on high speed until creamy. Add the remaining 1¼ cups water and blend briefly. Strain slowly through a fine sieve or cheesecloth into a large jug. Serve chilled.

Makes about 2 cups

SAUCES

We've included a large variety of sauces here that can be prepared ahead of time. Keep these sauces in glass or plastic containers in the refrigerator for up to a week, unless otherwise indicated. Take some to the office to use as spreads on rice cakes. They're great for combating sugar cravings and helping you through low-energy periods.

Sour Cream

¾ cup silken tofu, drained
2 tablespoons lemon juice
1 tablespoon tahini
3 teaspoons cider vinegar
1 tablespoon soy oil
Pinch of sea salt
2 tablespoons finely chopped fresh chives

In a steaming rack over a large pot of boiling water, steam the tofu for 2 minutes. In a blender or food processor, combine the tofu with the lemon juice, tahini, vinegar, oil, and salt. Process on high speed for 2 minutes. Sprinkle with the chives. Serve chilled.

Makes 1 cup

Sunflower Sour Cream

1¼ cups water
2 cups sunflower seeds
¼ cup lemon juice
1 teaspoon sea salt
½ teaspoon onion powder
½ teaspoon garlic powder

In a blender or food processor, combine the water, sunflower seeds, lemon juice, salt, onion powder, and garlic powder. Blend on high speed for 2 to 3 minutes, or until creamy. Serve chilled.

Makes 1 cup

Tofu Mayonnaise

1	cup firm tofu, drained and crumbled
¼	cup water
¼	cup canola oil
1	teaspoon lemon juice
1	teaspoon brewer's yeast (optional)
	Pinch of sea salt
½	teaspoon onion powder
½	teaspoon garlic powder
½	teaspoon cider vinegar

In a blender or food processor, combine the tofu, water, oil, lemon juice, yeast (if using), salt, onion powder, garlic powder, and vinegar. Blend on high speed for 3 to 4 minutes, or until creamy. If desired, add more salt to taste. Serve chilled.

Makes 1 cup

Almond Mayonnaise

2	cups toasted almonds
¾	cup soy milk
¼	teaspoon garlic powder
	Pinch of sea salt
1¼	cups safflower oil
3	tablespoons lemon juice
½	teaspoon cider vinegar

Remove the skins from the toasted almonds by rubbing them.

In a blender or food processor, grind the nuts into a fine paste. Add the soy milk, garlic powder, and salt. Blend until creamy.

With the blender or processor still running, add the oil in a slow, steady stream. (If the sauce has not thickened to your liking after you have poured the oil into the blender, pour the mixture into a large nonstick skillet and cook over medium heat, stirring constantly, until thickened. Remove from heat before adding the remaining ingredients.)

Add the lemon juice and vinegar in the same fashion as the oil and blend for another 2 minutes. Can be kept refrigerated for up to 10 days.

Makes 1 cup

Soy-Garlic Mayonnaise

¾   cup soy milk
½   teaspoon sea salt
2   cloves garlic, minced
¾   cup safflower oil
2   tablespoons lemon juice

In a blender or food processor, combine the soy milk, salt, and garlic. Blend until creamy. With the blender or processor still running, add the oil in a slow, steady stream. Add the lemon juice in the same fashion as the oil and blend for another 2 minutes. Serve chilled.

Makes 2½ cups

Tofu Cottage Cheese

2   cups firm tofu, drained
1   cup minced onions
1   tablespoon cider vinegar
2   tablespoons lemon juice
2   teaspoons parsley
     Pinch of sea salt

In a blender or food processor, combine 1 cup of the tofu with the onions, vinegar, lemon juice, parsley, and salt. Blend until smooth. Transfer the mixture into a large bowl.

In another small bowl, mash the remaining 1 cup tofu with a fork until crumbly. Add the tofu to the large bowl and mix well until mixture takes on the consistency of cottage cheese. Add salt to taste. Serve chilled.

Makes 2 cups

BASIC DIPS AND SPREADS

Dips are easy and healthy hors d'oeuvres for cocktail parties and everyday snacks. Cut up some celery, carrot, and cucumber sticks to dip. Spreads are great on rice cakes and oatmeal cakes. Make your own and keep in the refrigerator at home or in the office for up to a week unless otherwise indicated.

Hummus

1   tablespoon olive oil
1   cup finely chopped onions
4   cloves garlic, minced
2   cups cooked chickpeas
     Juice of 2 lemons
1½   cups tahini
¼   teaspoon ground red pepper
¼   cup cooking liquid from chickpeas

Heat the oil in a large nonstick skillet over medium heat. Add the onions and garlic. Sauté until tender.

In a blender or food processor, combine the chickpeas, lemon juice, tahini, red pepper, and reserved cooking liquid (or water if using canned beans). Blend on high speed until smooth and creamy.

Transfer the mixture into a medium bowl. Add the sautéed onions and mix well. Serve chilled.

Makes 2 cups

Variation: To make this into a dressing for salads or grains, increase the amount of cooking liquid gradually by tablespoons until it's a consistency you like. Blend the sautéed onions and garlic in the blender or processor with the rest of the mixture.

Guacamole

2	cups mashed ripe avocado
½	cup chopped cilantro
½	onion, finely chopped
2	cloves garlic, minced
1	cup finely chopped tomatoes
1	tablespoon lemon juice
½	teaspoon ground cumin
½	teaspoon ground red pepper
½	teaspoon sea salt
¼	cup minced fresh parsley

In a large bowl, combine the avocado, cilantro, onions, garlic, tomatoes, lemon juice, cumin, red pepper, salt, and parsley. Mix well. Serve immediately or keep refrigerated for up to 2 days.

Makes 2½ cups

Variation: For quick guacamole, use ½ teaspoon each onion and garlic powder and 2 tablespoons tomato puree instead of fresh onions, garlic, and tomatoes.

Salsa

This is a great dip for regular and blue corn tortilla chips.

4   plum tomatoes, diced
½   cup finely chopped red onions
1   green pepper, finely chopped
1   tablespoon minced garlic
2   teaspoons cider vinegar
2   teaspoons ground cumin
2   tablespoons minced fresh cilantro
1   red chili pepper, finely chopped (see note)
    Pinch of sea salt
    Pinch of ground black pepper

In a medium bowl, combine the tomatoes, onions, green peppers, garlic, vinegar, cumin, cilantro, chili peppers, salt, and black pepper. Mix well. Refrigerate for up to 2 days.

Makes 2 cups

Note: Wear plastic gloves when handling chili peppers.
Variation: If chili peppers are unbearably hot, add honey to taste to cool your taste buds.

Baba Ghannouj or "Eggplant Caviar"

1   medium eggplant
¼   cup lemon juice
¼   cup tahini
2   cloves garlic, minced
1   tablespoon olive oil
    Pinch of sea salt
    Pinch of ground black pepper
¼   cup minced fresh parsley
2   scallions, finely chopped

Preheat the oven to 200°F. Using a fork, prick the eggplant all over then place it into a deep baking dish. Bake for about 45 minutes, or until crinkly on the outside and soft on the inside. Allow the eggplant to cool until you can handle it safely. Remove the skin and scoop out the inside.

In a blender or food processor, chop or puree the eggplant with the lemon juice, tahini, garlic, oil, salt, and pepper. Chill the mixture. Top with the parsley and scallions when ready to serve.

Makes 2 cups

Variation: The eggplant can also be char-grilled on a skewer over an open flame. This gives it a distinct and delicious smoky taste.

Artichoke Spread

7   artichokes
2   tablespoons olive oil
1   tablespoon wine vinegar
2   cloves garlic, minced
1   tablespoon lemon juice
   Pinch of sea salt
   Pinch of ground black pepper
   Toast

Remove the stalks and the tough outer leaves from the artichokes. Place them in a large pot of boiling water and boil gently for 45 minutes. Remove them from the water and allow to cool.

Discard the remaining tough leaves. Scrape the soft, edible flesh from the bottom of the leaves into a blender or food processor. Scoop out the chokes and discard. Add the soft artichoke centers to the blender or processor. Add the oil, vinegar, garlic, lemon juice, salt, and pepper. Blend on high speed until smooth and creamy. Chill and serve on toast.

Makes 2 cups

SALAD DRESSINGS
AND TOPPINGS

Following is a variety of dressings to use for salads or with any cooked grains—millet, quinoa, barley, rice, or kashi. They can all be made ahead of time and refrigerated. They are also more expensive. Keep these dressings at the office, too, for topping salad bar fare.

Thousand Island Dressing

¾ cup Tofu Mayonnaise (see page 69)
¼ cup ketchup
1 tablespoon finely chopped scallions
2 teaspoons finely chopped fresh parsley
1 tablespoon grated green peppers
2 tablespoons grated dill pickles
1 teaspoon lemon juice

In a blender or food processor, combine the mayonnaise, ketchup, scallions, parsley, peppers, pickles, and lemon juice. Blend until smooth and creamy. Keep refrigerated.

Makes about 1¼ cups

Variation: Add chopped black olives and grated carrots for a delicious twist to this classic recipe.

French Dressing

½ cup vegetable juice or water
¼ cup extra-virgin olive oil
¼ cup finely chopped fresh parsley
1 clove garlic, minced

(continued)

1½   teaspoons Dijon mustard
2   tablespoons lemon juice
1   tablespoon honey
     Pinch of sea salt
     Pinch of ground black pepper

In a blender or food processor, combine the vegetable juice or water, oil, parsley, garlic, mustard, lemon juice, honey, salt, and pepper. Blend at high speed until creamy. Keep refrigerated.

Makes 1¼ cups

Italian Dressing

½   cup water or tomato juice
¼   cup extra-virgin olive oil
1   tablespoon lemon juice
1   clove garlic, crushed
1   tablespoon minced onions
1   tablespoon fresh basil strips
1   teaspoon oregano
1   tablespoon tomato puree
1   tablespoon balsamic vinegar

In a large bowl, combine the water or tomato juice, oil, lemon juice, garlic, onions, basil, oregano, tomato puree, and vinegar. Mix together well with a whisk. Keep refrigerated.

Makes 1¼ cups

Garlic and Tahini Dressing

¼   cup tahini
½   cup + 2 tablespoons water
1½   tablespoons extra-virgin olive oil
1   clove garlic, minced
2   tablespoons lemon or lime juice

1 tablespoon soy sauce
1 tablespoon cider vinegar
Pinch of ground black pepper
Fresh mixed herbs

In a large bowl, combine the tahini, water, oil, garlic, lemon or lime juice, soy sauce, vinegar, and pepper. Whisk together until well-mixed. Keep refrigerated. Add the fresh herbs, to taste, just before serving.

Makes 1¾ cups

Carrot and Ginger Dressing

¾ cup carrot juice
3 tablespoons tahini
2 teaspoons lemon juice
2 tablespoons chopped fresh cilantro
2 tablespoons sesame oil (optional)
¾ teaspoon honey or maple syrup
½ teaspoon grated fresh ginger
½ teaspoon curry powder
Pinch of sea salt
Pinch of ground black pepper

In a blender or food processor, combine the carrot juice, tahini, lemon juice, cilantro, oil (if using), honey or syrup, ginger, curry, salt, and pepper. Blend well. Keep refrigerated.

Makes 1 cup

Green Dressing

1 plum tomato, finely chopped
1 cup finely chopped fresh arugula or spinach
¼ cup water or vegetable juice
¼ cup extra-virgin olive oil
2 tablespoons lemon juice

(continued)

    2   cloves garlic, crushed
    2   tablespoons soy sauce
    2   teaspoons honey
    1   teaspoon chopped fresh oregano
         Pinch of sea salt
         Pinch of ground black pepper

In a blender or food processor, combine the tomatoes, arugula or spinach, water or vegetable juice, oil, lemon juice, garlic, soy sauce, honey, oregano, salt, and pepper. Blend until smooth and creamy. If the dressing is too thick, strain it through a fine sieve. Keep refrigerated.

Makes 1¼ cups

Sweet and Gingery Dressing

    2   tablespoons walnut oil
    6   shallots, peeled and finely chopped
    ¼   cup finely chopped fresh mint
    ¼   cup pineapple juice
    ¼   cup water
    1   tablespoon grated fresh ginger
    1   teaspoon rice vinegar
         Pinch of sea salt
         Pinch of ground black pepper

In a large nonstick skillet, warm the oil over medium heat. Add the shallots and sauté for 5 to 6 minutes. Transfer the shallots to a blender or food processor. Add the mint, pineapple juice, water, ginger, vinegar, salt, and pepper. Blend on high speed until smooth. Keep refrigerated.

Makes 1 cup

Sunflower Dressing

    2   large tomatoes, skinned and seeded
    ¼   cup sun-dried tomatoes
    ¼   cup toasted sunflower seeds

¼   cup orange juice
¼   cup water
¼   teaspoon honey
¼   teaspoon mustard
¼   teaspoon soy sauce
     Pinch of ground black pepper

In a blender or food processor, combine the skinned and the sun-dried tomatoes. Blend briefly. Add the sunflower seeds, orange juice, water, honey, mustard, soy sauce, and pepper. Blend until minced but not smooth. Keep refrigerated.

Makes 1¼ cups

Creamy Mustard Dressing

½   cup firm tofu, drained and crumbled
¼   cup + 2 tablespoons extra-virgin olive oil
¼   cup vegetable juice or water
3   scallions, finely chopped
1   stalk celery, finely chopped
1   clove garlic, minced
3   tablespoons lemon juice
2   tablespoons ketchup or tomato puree
1   tablespoon cider vinegar
2   teaspoons soy sauce
1   teaspoon mustard
     Chopped fresh chives or dill
     Pinch of sea salt
     Pinch of ground black pepper

In a blender or food processor, combine the tofu, oil, vegetable juice or water, scallions, celery, garlic, lemon juice, ketchup or tomato puree, vinegar, soy sauce, mustard, chives or dill, salt, and pepper. Blend until smooth and creamy. Keep refrigerated.

Makes 1¼ cups

Note: Adding a little more vegetable juice or water will change the consistency for other uses.

Mango and Ginger Salad Dressing

½   cup mango juice
¼   cup diced fresh mango
¼   cup water
2   tablespoons minced scallions
1   teaspoon juice of freshly grated ginger
1   teaspoon fresh lime juice
¼   teaspoon ground red pepper
1   tablespoon fresh coriander
    Pinch of sea salt

In a blender or food processor, combine the mango juice, mango, water, scallions, ginger juice, lime juice, pepper, coriander, and salt. Blend well until smooth. Keep refrigerated.

Makes 1¼ cups

Walnut Oil and Fresh Juice Dressing

¼   cup + 1 tablespoon orange juice
¼   cup + 1 tablespoon grapefruit juice
¼   cup water
3   scallions, finely chopped
1   tablespoon walnut oil
1   teaspoon champagne vinegar
½   teaspoon grated lemon rind
¼   teaspoon crushed dill seeds
    Fresh herbs
    Pinch of sea salt
    Pinch of ground black pepper

In a large bowl, combine the orange juice, grapefruit juice, water, scallions, oil, vinegar, lemon rind, dill seeds, herbs, salt, and pepper. Whisk together well. Keep refrigerated.

Makes about 1 cup

Roasted Red Pepper Topping

 1   large sweet red pepper
10   golden raisins, soaked in hot water and drained
 ¼   cup water
 1   clove garlic, minced
 1   tablespoon extra-virgin olive oil
 1   teaspoon sherry vinegar
 1   teaspoon chopped fresh basil
 1   teaspoon chopped fresh oregano
     Pinch of sea salt
     Pinch of ground black pepper

Preheat the broiler.

In a large broiling pan, broil the pepper about 4" from the heat for about 3 minutes, turning it so that all sides are evenly charred. Place the pepper in a covered container for about 5 minutes; the moisture released by its heat will make the skin easier to remove. Using a paring knife, peel the skin off and remove the seeds and ribs.

Put the pepper into a blender or food processor. Add the raisins, water, garlic, oil, vinegar, basil, oregano, salt, and black pepper. Blend until smooth. Keep refrigerated.

Makes ¾ cup

Creamy Oriental Dressing

 ¼   cup light sesame oil
 ¼   cup pine nuts
 2   tablespoons unsweetened shredded coconut
1½   tablespoons water
 1   tablespoon chopped fresh cilantro
 1   teaspoon minced fresh ginger
 1   teaspoon soy sauce
 1   teaspoon lemon juice

In a blender or food processor, combine the oil, nuts, coconut, water, cilantro, ginger, soy sauce, and lemon juice. Blend until creamy. Keep refrigerated.

Makes 1 cup

Tofu Russian Dressing

1 cup firm tofu, drained and crumbled
¼ cup ketchup
¼ cup lemon juice
⅛ cup grated carrots
⅛ cup grated parsley
1 tablespoon tahini
1 teaspoon dried dill

In a blender or food processor, blend the tofu until smooth. Add the ketchup, lemon juice, carrots, parsley, tahini, and dill. Blend until creamy. Serve chilled.

Makes 1 cup

Cucumber and Dill Dressing

1 cucumber, peeled and cut into 4" slices
½ cup chopped fresh dill
¼ cup water
2 cloves garlic, minced
2 tablespoons nondairy sour cream
¼ teaspoon mustard powder
1 tablespoon minced red onions
Pinch of sea salt
Pinch of ground black pepper

In a blender or food processor, combine the cucumbers, dill, water, garlic, sour cream, mustard powder, onions, salt, and pepper. Blend until smooth and creamy. Keep refrigerated.

Makes 1¼ cups

Tomato Dressing

  ½ cup tomato juice
  ¼ cup water
  1 clove garlic, minced
  1 tablespoon chopped fresh basil
  1 tablespoon mustard
  ½ teaspoon honey
  Pinch of sea salt
  Pinch of ground black pepper

In a blender or food processor, combine the tomato juice, water, garlic, basil, mustard, honey, salt, and pepper. Blend until creamy. Keep refrigerated.

Makes 1¼ cups

Lemon Vinaigrette

  ¼ cup + 2 tablespoons extra-virgin olive oil
  ¼ cup water
  3 tablespoons lemon juice
  2 tablespoons nondairy sour cream or mayonnaise
  1 tablespoon sherry vinegar
  1 teaspoon mustard
  ½ teaspoon chopped fresh tarragon
  Pinch of sea salt
  Pinch of ground black pepper

In a medium bowl, combine the oil, water, lemon juice, sour cream or mayonnaise, vinegar, mustard, tarragon, salt, and pepper. Whisk together until well-mixed. Keep refrigerated.

Makes ¾ cup

Caper and Black Olive Dressing

  1 large sweet red pepper
  3 scallions, finely chopped
  ½ cup pitted and sliced black olives

(continued)

¼   cup water
1   clove garlic, minced
1   tablespoon chopped small capers
1   tablespoon finely chopped fresh parsley
1   tablespoon balsamic vinegar
1   teaspoon onion powder

Preheat the broiler.

In a large broiling pan, broil the pepper about 4" from the heat for about 3 minutes, turning it so that all sides are evenly charred. Place the pepper in a covered container for about 5 minutes; the moisture released by its heat will make the skin easier to remove. Using a paring knife, peel the skin off and remove the seeds and ribs.

In a blender or food processor, puree the pepper.

In a medium bowl, combine the pureed pepper, scallions, olives, water, garlic, capers, parsley, vinegar, and onion powder. Whisk together until well-mixed. Keep refrigerated.

Makes ¾ cup

Beet and Horseradish Dressing

¼   cup extra-virgin olive oil
¼   cup water
1   medium beet, cooked and shredded
1   tablespoon wine vinegar
1   teaspoon chopped fresh horseradish
1   tablespoon white sesame seeds, toasted
   Fresh herbs
   Pinch of sea salt
   Pinch of ground black pepper

In a blender or food processor, combine the oil, water, beets, vinegar, and horseradish. Blend together well. Blend in the sesame seeds, herbs, salt, and pepper right before serving. Keep refrigerated.

Makes ¾ cup

Peanut and Coconut Sauce

¼   cup coconut cream
¼   cup water
2   tablespoons vegetable stock
2   teaspoons soy sauce
1   tablespoon crunchy peanut butter
2   teaspoons minced scallions
1   teaspoon minced fresh ginger

In a medium bowl, combine the coconut cream, water, stock, soy sauce, peanut butter, scallions, and ginger. Whisk together until smooth. Keep refrigerated.

Makes ¾ cup

Creamy Spinach Dressing

8   medium spinach leaves, chopped
½   cup soy cream
¼   cup + 2 tablespoons extra-virgin olive oil or walnut oil
1   clove garlic, minced
2   tablespoons finely chopped fresh parsley
2   tablespoons lemon juice
1   teaspoon honey
1   tablespoon coarsely chopped walnuts

In a blender or food processor, combine the spinach, soy cream, oil, garlic, parsley, lemon juice, honey, and nuts. Blend together well. Keep refrigerated.

Makes ¾ cup

Pesto and Carrot Dressing

½   cup fresh carrot juice
¼   cup ready-made pesto
¼   cup soy milk

(continued)

¼   cup coarsely chopped walnuts
2   tablespoons extra-virgin olive oil (optional)
½   teaspoon soy sauce
    Pinch of ground black pepper

In a medium bowl, combine the carrot juice, pesto, soy milk, nuts, oil (if using), soy sauce, and pepper. Whisk together. Keep refrigerated.

Makes 1¼ cups

Japanese Plum Dressing

¼   cup water
1   small tomato, finely chopped
2   scallions, finely chopped
2   tablespoons sesame oil
1   teaspoon umeboshi plum paste
1   tablespoon mirin
1   tablespoon soy sauce
½   teaspoon finely chopped fresh ginger
    Chopped fresh parsley

In a medium bowl, combine the water, tomatoes, scallions, oil, plum paste, mirin, soy sauce, ginger, and parsley. Whisk together. Keep refrigerated.

Makes ¾ cup

Variation: For added flavor, sprinkle with black sesame seeds and nori (dried seaweed) flakes.

Miso and Ginger Dressing

2   tablespoons red miso paste
2   tablespoons tahini
1½   tablespoons water
1   tablespoon mirin
½   teaspoon chopped fresh ginger
1   tablespoon gomasio
1½   teaspoons soy sauce

In a medium bowl, combine the miso paste, tahini, water, mirin, ginger, gomasio, and soy sauce. Whisk together. Keep refrigerated.

Makes ¾ cup

Pumpkin Seed Dressing

1 cup finely chopped fresh parsley
¼ cup pumpkin seeds
⅓ cup water
2 tablespoons lemon juice
1 clove garlic, finely chopped
1 tablespoon sunflower oil
  Pinch of sea salt
  Pinch of ground black pepper

In a blender or food processor, combine the parsley, pumpkin seeds, water, lemon juice, garlic, oil, salt, and pepper. Blend until smooth and creamy. Add more or less water to adjust consistency. Keep refrigerated.

Makes ¾ cup

Curry Dressing

2 cloves garlic, crushed
¼ cup extra-virgin olive oil
¼ cup water
2 tablespoons tahini
1 tablespoon lemon juice
1 teaspoon finely chopped fresh ginger
½ teaspoon ground cumin
½ teaspoon chopped fresh cilantro
½ teaspoon curry powder
  Pinch of sea salt
  Pinch of ground black pepper

In a medium bowl, combine the garlic, oil, water, tahini, lemon juice, ginger, cumin, cilantro, curry, salt, and pepper. Whisk together. Keep refrigerated.

Makes ¾ cup

STOCKS

Here are two recipes for good everyday stocks. You can change the vegetables in the recipe for the basic stock according to the seasons, like adding pumpkin in autumn or seasonal greens.

Basic Stock

2	medium onions, quartered
2	medium carrots, cut into 1" pieces
2	medium leeks, chopped
1	large potato, cubed
2	cloves garlic, chopped
	Handful of greens or mushroom stems
1	bay leaf
4	peppercorns
2	cloves
1	bunch fresh parsley, stemmed and chopped
½	teaspoon chopped fresh marjoram
½	teaspoon chopped fresh thyme
1	teaspoon sea salt
4	cups water

In a large pot, combine the onions, carrots, leeks, potatoes, garlic, greens or mushrooms, bay leaf, peppercorns, cloves, parsley, marjoram, thyme, and salt. Cover with the water and bring to a boil over medium heat. Simmer, covered, for 45 minutes to 1½ hours, stirring occasionally.

Remove from the heat and let cool to room temperature. Strain through a sieve. For a more potent stock, simmer the broth until it is reduced by half. This stock can be refrigerated for up to 5 days.

Makes 4 cups

Variations: For a richer stock, sauté vegetables in 2 tablespoons extra-virgin olive oil before adding them to the pot.

To sweeten the stock, add slices of apples and pears.

To make Curry Stock: Add 1 teaspoon each ground cilantro, cumin, and turmeric.

To make Mediterranean Stock: Add more parsley and garlic, 1 teaspoon fresh pesto, and ½ cup white wine.

To make Tomato Soup: Reduce the water and add 4 cups chopped fresh tomatoes and some mirin.

To make Mushroom Soup: Add 1 cup fresh shiitake mushrooms, 1 cup button mushrooms, and ⅔ cup white wine.

Japanese Stock

1	piece kombu (about 8"), cut into 1" strips (see note)
4	dried shiitake mushrooms
4	cups warm water
1	carrot, finely chopped
4	scallions, finely chopped
2	tablespoons sea salt
3	tablespoons soy sauce
2	tablespoons sugar
2	tablespoons mirin
2	teaspoons sake
1	teaspoon wasabi paste

In a large pot, soak the kombu and mushrooms in the warm water for 2 to 3 hours. Bring the water to a boil over medium heat. Reduce the heat. Add the carrots, scallions, salt, soy sauce, sugar, mirin, sake, and wasabi paste. Simmer for 15 to 20 minutes. Keep refrigerated for up to 5 days.

Makes 4 cups

Note: Kombu comes with a natural, white powder covering that has lots of flavor. Its surface should be wiped off, not washed, before it is added to the stock.

Variation: To make Thai Stock: Add 1 teaspoon each grated fresh ginger, lemon grass, sweet basil, and red chili peppers.

BASIC PASTRY RECIPES

Here are some simple pastry recipes for the basic pie crust and pizza shell.

Pie Crust

> 1¾ cups whole-wheat pastry flour
> Pinch of sea salt
> ¼ cup + 2 tablespoons soy margarine, chilled
> ¼ cup iced water

In a large bowl, sift together the flour and salt. Add the soy margarine by grating it or by cutting it into the flour with 2 knives until the mixture resembles bread crumbs.

Using your hands or a fork to mix, gradually add the water, 1 tablespoon at a time, mixing until the dough forms into a ball. Be careful not to overhandle it.

Wrap the dough in waxed paper and place it inside a resealable plastic storage bag. Refrigerate for up to a week.

Roll out the dough to fit a 9" pie plate. Place the dough in the plate and flute the edges. For best results, freeze the shaped dough for at least 1 hour before baking it.

If baking without a filling, preheat the oven to 350°F. Cook the frozen pie crust in the hot oven for 15 to 20 minutes, or until lightly browned. The crust can be lined with foil to keep it from cracking and the center filled with dried beans to weigh it down and prevent it from becoming soggy.

Makes 1 single-layer crust

Whole-Wheat Pizza Dough

1¼ tablespoons dried yeast
¼ cup + 2 tablespoons warm water
Pinch of sugar
1¾ cups whole-wheat flour
2 cups unbleached white flour
½ teaspoon sea salt
3 tablespoons extra-virgin olive oil

In a medium bowl, combine the yeast, water, and sugar. Stir well to dissolve and activate the yeast.

On a clean working surface, mix together the whole-wheat flour and the white flour and make a small well in the center. Pour in the yeast mix, the salt, and 1 tablespoon of the oil. With your hands, start sifting flour into the well carefully, kneading until the dough becomes a ball. Continue kneading for another 8 to 10 minutes, or until the dough is moist and elastic. Add more water, if needed, as you work with the dough.

In a large bowl, add 1 tablespoon of the oil, turning the bowl to allow the oil to coat the inside. Place the dough in the oiled bowl, turning it over once so that all sides are coated. Cover the dough with a clean towel and keep it in a warm place, preferably in the sun. Let the dough rise for approximately 60 to 80 minutes, or until it doubles in size.

Preheat the oven to 350°F.

If using a pizza pan, oil the pan well with the remaining 1 tablespoon oil. Roll out the pizza dough on a floured surface to half of its final size.

Place the dough in the pan and slowly stretch it to the sides and over the borders (the best size is 12" round and about ¾" thick). Top it with your favorite ingredients and bake for 30 minutes.

Makes 1 crust

BREAKFAST

These recipes will make nice substitutes for the more fat-filled muffin recipes you may be using now.

Apple-Cinnamon Muffins

¼	cup sunflower oil
¼	cup honey
¾	cup applesauce
2	cups whole-wheat flour
½	teaspoon baking soda
1½	teaspoons baking powder
¾	teaspoon ground allspice
¼	teaspoon ground cinnamon
½	teaspoon sea salt
½	cup raisins

Preheat the oven to 350°F. Lightly-coat a 12-cup muffin tin with nonstick cooking spray.

In a small bowl, mix the oil, honey, and applesauce well.

In a large bowl, sift together the flour, baking soda, baking powder, allspice, cinnamon, and salt. Stir the wet ingredients into the dry, adding the raisins. Don't overmix; the mixture should be lumpy. Spoon the batter into the muffin cups, filling each cup about three-fourths full.

Bake for 20 minutes, or until a toothpick inserted in the center of a muffin comes out clean. Remove the muffins from the tin and cool on a wire rack.

Makes 12

Note: To help keep the muffins moist, put an ovenproof bowl filled with water in the oven while the muffins bake.

Banana and Bran Muffins

2	egg whites or 1 whole egg
1¼	cups mashed ripe bananas
¼	cup sunflower oil
¼	cup + 1 tablespoon maple syrup
2	tablespoons mashed tofu
1¼	cups whole-wheat flour
¾	cup oat bran
2	teaspoons baking powder
½	teaspoon baking soda
	Pinch of sea salt
	Pinch of ground cinnamon
	Pinch of nutmeg or a few cloves

Preheat the oven to 350°F. Lightly coat a 12-cup muffin tin with nonstick cooking spray.

In a blender or food processor, combine the egg whites or egg, bananas, oil, syrup, and tofu. Blend well on high speed.

In a large bowl, sift together the flour, oat bran, baking powder, baking soda, salt, cinnamon, and nutmeg or cloves. Make a well in the center of the dry ingredients. Pour the banana mixture into the well, folding together with a spatula until thoroughly mixed. Spoon the batter into the muffin cups, filling each cup about three-fourths full.

Bake for 25 minutes, or until a toothpick inserted in the center of a muffin comes out clean. Remove the muffins from the tin and cool on a wire rack.

Makes 12 to 14

Walnut and Date Muffins

3	cups whole-wheat flour
1¼	cups unbleached white flour
1	tablespoon baking powder

(continued)

```
        Pinch of sea salt
  4     egg whites
  ¾     cup soy milk
  ½     cup sunflower oil
  ½     cup honey
  1¼    cups chopped dates
  1     cup chopped walnuts
```

Preheat the oven to 350°F. Lightly coat a 12-cup muffin tin with nonstick cooking spray.

In a medium bowl, sift together the whole-wheat and white flours, baking powder, and salt.

In a large bowl, whisk together the egg whites, soy milk, oil, and honey. Fold the dry ingredients into the wet ingredients, stirring in the dates and walnuts, until well-mixed. Spoon the batter into the muffin cups, filling each cup about three-fourths full.

Bake for 25 minutes, or until a toothpick inserted in the center of a muffin comes out clean. Remove the muffins from the tin and cool on a wire rack.

Makes 12

Cracked-Wheat Porridge

```
  1     cup cracked wheat
  3½    cups vanilla-flavored soy milk
  2½    cups water
  ½     cup golden raisins
  3     tablespoons honey
  ¼     cup toasted almonds
  ¼     cup chopped apricots
```

In a large saucepan, cook the cracked wheat over medium heat, stirring constantly, until lightly brown. Add 2 cups of the soy milk and 2 cups of the water. Stir in the raisins. Mix well and bring to a boil.

Reduce the heat. Cover and let simmer, stirring often, for 15 minutes, or until all the moisture is absorbed. Turn off the heat and leave covered for 10 minutes.

In a medium saucepan, warm the remaining 1½ cups soy milk. Add the remaining ½ cup water, the honey, and the almonds. Pour over the porridge and top with the apricots. Serve warm.

Makes 4 servings

Fig and Oat Porridge

¾ cup raw oat groats, soaked for 48 hours
5 figs, soaked overnight
Unsweetened shredded coconut

Preheat the oven to 325°F. Lightly coat a deep baking dish with nonstick cooking spray.

In a blender or food processor, combine the drained groats and figs. Blend until smooth.

Pour the groat mixture into the prepared baking dish and sprinkle with the coconut. Bake for 1 hour, or until lightly browned.

Makes 3½ cups

Brown Rice Porridge

1 cup cooked brown rice
1 cup cooked barley
2 cups nut or soy milk
1 cup chopped mixed nuts
½ cup golden raisins
¼ cup chopped dates
½ teaspoon lemon juice

(continued)

2 tablespoons honey
Pinch of sea salt
Pinch of ground cinnamon
½ teaspoon vanilla

Preheat the oven to 350°F. Lightly coat a deep baking dish with nonstick cooking spray.

In a large bowl, combine the rice, barley, and nut or soy milk. Mix well. Stir in the nuts, raisins, dates, lemon juice, honey, salt, cinnamon, and vanilla until well-mixed.

Pour the mixture into the baking dish. Bake for 45 to 60 minutes, depending on the desired consistency. To keep it creamy, add more milk.

Makes 4 cups

Granola / Muesli

3 cups rolled oats
1½ cups chopped almonds
½ cup unsweetened shredded coconut
½ cup pumpkin seeds
¼ cup sunflower oil
½ cup maple syrup
1 teaspoon vanilla
½ teaspoon almond extract
1 teaspoon ground cinnamon
Pinch of sea salt
2 cups mixed dried fruit, such as apricots, prunes, figs, papaya, mango

Preheat the oven to 325°F.

In a medium bowl, combine the oats, almonds, coconut, and pumpkin seeds. Mix well.

In a medium saucepan, combine the oil, syrup, vanilla, almond extract, cinnamon, and salt. Mix well. Warm over medium heat until watery.

Pour the wet mixture over the dry ingredients and mix until everything is moistened. (It is best mixed by your hands.)

Spread the mixture onto a baking sheet and bake for 20 minutes, stirring every 5 minutes, until evenly golden. Transfer to a tray or a bowl and toss until cool.

Add the dried fruit and store in an airtight container.

Makes about 6 cups

Waffles

2	cups whole-wheat flour
¾	cup unbleached white flour
¼	cup rice flour
3	teaspoons baking powder
¼	teaspoon sea salt
4	egg whites, beaten
1½	cups soy milk
1	teaspoon vanilla
¾	cup sunflower oil

Preheat a waffle iron. Liberally coat the iron with nonstick cooking spray.

In a medium bowl, mix together the whole-wheat, white, and rice flours with the baking powder and salt. Stir in the egg whites, soy milk, and vanilla, adding the oil last. Don't overmix.

Pour the batter onto the hot waffle iron and close the lid. Cook for 6 to 7 minutes, or until golden brown. Serve warm.

Makes 4 to 5

Note: Top with maple syrup or butter and chopped fresh fruits and nuts.

Pancakes

  4   cups soy milk
  2   tablespoons honey
  ½   cup poppy seeds
  3   cups whole-wheat flour
  ½   teaspoon baking soda
  1   teaspoon sea salt
  4   egg whites, beaten
  2   tablespoons sunflower oil
  1   tablespoon maple flavoring

In a medium saucepan, warm 2 cups of the soy milk over medium heat. As it reaches a boil, add the honey and poppy seeds. Remove from the heat and set aside to cool.

Lightly coat a large skillet with nonstick cooking spray. Warm the pan over medium heat.

In a large bowl, mix together the flour, baking soda, and salt. Gradually stir in the milk mixture, the remaining 2 cups milk, the egg whites, the sunflower oil, and the maple flavoring.

Add several spoonfuls of batter to the heated pan, spreading the batter with the bottom of a round spoon. When the edges are cooked and the bottom is brown, flip and cook the other side for another 2 to 3 minutes. Serve warm.

Makes 15 to 18

Note: Top with warmed maple syrup, any fresh fruit topping, or soy cream.

Sumptuous Sunday Breakfast

Baked Eggs

These eggs make a great breakfast when served with the following Sautéed Tomatoes and Mushrooms and Hash Brown Waffles recipes.

    2 tablespoons ketchup
    2 teaspoons mustard
    2 scallions, finely chopped
    3 eggs
       Pinch of sea salt
       Pinch of ground black pepper
       Chopped fresh cilantro

Preheat the oven to 350°F. Lightly coat 2 or 3 cups in a muffin tin with nonstick cooking spray.

In a small bowl, mix the ketchup, mustard, and scallions. Spoon this mixture evenly into the prepared muffin cups. Crack an egg on top of the ketchup mixture in each cup. Sprinkle lightly with the salt, pepper, and cilantro.

Bake for 8 to 10 minutes, depending on how you like your eggs. When ready, use a knife to turn them out onto a hot plate. Serve warm.

Makes 3

Sautéed Tomatoes and Mushrooms

    2   tablespoons olive oil
    1½   cups quartered mushrooms
    1   teaspoon sea salt
    1   teaspoon ground black pepper
    1   teaspoon chopped fresh parsley
    2   tomatoes, halved

In a large skillet, warm 1 tablespoon of the oil over medium heat. Add the mushrooms, salt, pepper, and ½ teaspoon of the parsley. Sauté until lightly browned.

Move the mushroom mixture to one side of the pan and add the tomatoes. Drizzle the tomatoes with the remaining 1 tablespoon oil and ½ teaspoon parsley. Toss together and serve warm.

Makes 2 servings

Hash Brown Waffles

2	tablespoons olive oil
1	onion, finely chopped
1	teaspoon dried dill
2	pounds potatoes, shredded
	Handful of fresh parsley, finely chopped
	Pinch of sea salt
	Pinch of ground black pepper

Preheat a waffle iron. Liberally coat the iron with nonstick cooking spray.

In a large skillet, warm the oil. Add the onions and dill. Sauté for 5 minutes. Mix in the potatoes, parsley, salt, and pepper. Cook for 5 minutes, or until potatoes are partially cooked.

Transfer the potato mixture onto the hot waffle iron. Close the lid of the waffle iron and cook for 10 to 12 minutes, or until browned.

Makes 2 servings

High-Protein Vegan Breakfast

Scrambled Tofu

For maximum protein, serve this dish with the Baked Beans and Savory Flaked Puffed Rice recipes below.

2	tablespoons olive oil
¾	cup finely chopped onions
1	clove garlic, chopped
¼	teaspoon curry powder (optional)
1	carrot, grated
1	stalk celery, thinly sliced
¼	teaspoon sea salt
¼	teaspoon ground black pepper
¼	cup diced fresh tomatoes
2	cups crumbled firm tofu
1	tablespoon chopped fresh parsley

In a large skillet, warm the oil over medium heat. Add the onions and garlic. Sauté for 3 to 5 minutes, or until translucent. Add the curry (if using), carrots, and celery. Cook for 3 to 4 minutes more. Sprinkle with the salt and pepper. Continue cooking until vegetables are almost soft. Add the tomatoes and tofu and stir well or use a potato masher to combine. Continue cooking until ingredients are dry. Sprinkle with the parsley and serve warm.

Makes 2 servings

Baked Beans

This is great served on whole-wheat toast.

2	tablespoons olive oil
1	onion, diced
1	clove garlic, chopped

(continued)

2   tablespoons firm tofu, drained and mashed
2   cups cooked navy beans (reserve 1 cup of the cooking
     liquid)
¼   cup chopped pimientos
2   tablespoons tomato puree
1   teaspoon mustard
     Pinch of sea salt
     Pinch of ground black pepper
1   teaspoon honey
     Gomasio

Preheat the oven to 350°F.

In a medium skillet, warm the oil over medium heat. Add the onions, garlic, and tofu. Sauté for 2 minutes. Remove from the heat.

In a large bowl, combine the beans, pimientos, tomato puree, mustard, salt, pepper, and honey. Mix well. Stir in the sautéed tofu mixture, adding 1 tablespoon at a time of the cooking water from the beans so that the mixture is not too dry.

Transfer the beans to a baking dish, cover, and bake for 30 minutes. Uncover, add more cooking water if dry, and cook for another 15 minutes. Sprinkle with the gomasio.

Makes 2 servings

Savory Flaked Puffed Rice

2   tablespoons vegetable oil
1   teaspoon mustard seeds
1   onion, sliced
¼   teaspoon turmeric
¼   teaspoon dried coriander
1   carrot, diced
1½ cups green peas or small cauliflower florets
     Water

1   cup puffed rice (see note)
¼   teaspoon curry powder
     Pinch of sea salt
     Pinch of ground black pepper
¼   cup chopped roasted peanuts
1   tablespoon chopped fresh cilantro
2   tablespoons lemon juice

In a large wok or skillet over medium heat, warm the oil. Add the mustard seeds. Reduce the heat and cover until the seeds stop spluttering. Add the onions, turmeric, and coriander. Sauté until translucent. Add the carrots and green peas or cauliflower, with a splash of water. Mix well and cook for 6 to 8 minutes.

In a small bowl, soak the puffed rice in cold water for 5 minutes. Drain and add to the wok or skillet. Sprinkle the vegetables with the curry, salt, and pepper. Mix well. Cook for another 8 minutes, stirring frequently. Sprinkle with the peanuts, cilantro, and lemon juice. Serve warm.

Makes 2 servings

Note: Puffed rice is available at health food stores.

FRUIT BREAKFASTS

Fruit breakfasts are deliciously light and provide all the sweetness that you crave in the morning. Always choose fruits that are in season, and drink a fruit or vegetable juice cocktail each morning for a vitamin-packed start to your days.

Fruit Salad with Mint

     Seasonal fruit, peeled and thinly sliced
¾   cup plain or soy yogurt
2–3   mint leaves, torn

In a large bowl, combine the fruit and yogurt. Mix well. Sprinkle with the mint leaves. The juice from the fruit will make this mixture creamy and light.

Makes 2 servings

Strawberries and Nut Cream

½   cup soy cream
¼   cup finely chopped hazelnuts, almonds, or walnuts
2   cups strawberries

In a blender or food processor, combine the soy cream and nuts. Blend until smooth and creamy. Pour over the strawberries.

Makes 2 servings

Variation: For a different light summer breakfast, pour natural maple syrup on raspberries, blueberries, loganberries, blackberries, red currants, or black currants. Pick firm berries, as they are sweetest.

Apple, Celery, and Nut Delight

1½   apples, finely sliced
1   stalk celery, finely chopped
¾   cup plain or soy yogurt
½   cup finely chopped hazelnuts, almonds, or walnuts

In a large bowl, combine the apples, celery, yogurt, and nuts. Mix thoroughly. Serve chilled.

Makes 2 servings

DESSERT

The following dessert suggestions should please even the most finicky sweet tooth.

Brown Rice Pudding

 1   cup brown rice
 3   cups vanilla-flavored soy milk
 1   cinnamon stick
 ¼   cup golden raisins
 ¼   cup chopped apricots
 ¼   cup slivered almonds

Preheat the oven to 350°F.

In a fine sieve, rinse and drain the rice well.

In a large saucepan, combine the rice, soy milk, and cinnamon stick. On medium-low heat, gently simmer for 1 hour. Stir in the raisins, apricots, and almonds. Remove the cinnamon stick and transfer the rice to a baking dish. Bake for 25 minutes. Serve warm or at room temperature.

Makes 2 servings

Firnee

 2½   cups vanilla-flavored soy milk
 ⅛   teaspoon cardamom seeds, crushed
 ¼   cup maple syrup
 3   tablespoons soy milk
 5   teaspoons rice flour
 2   tablespoons chopped mixed nuts

In a medium saucepan, warm the vanilla-flavored soy milk over medium heat, stirring constantly. Add the cardamom seeds and syrup. Stir well and bring to a boil. Remove from the heat.

In a large bowl, combine the soy milk and rice flour. Mix well. Add the heated milk mixture in a slow, thin stream. Whisk together until well-mixed.

Return the mixture to the saucepan and cook for 15 minutes on low heat. Remove from the heat and pour into individual bowls. Sprinkle with the nuts and allow to cool. Serve chilled or at room temperature.

Makes 2 servings

Strawberry Couscous Cake

This cake is also delicious topped with other seasonal berries, such as blueberries and raspberries.

Couscous Cake

1¼	cups couscous
1¾	cups almond amazake
¾	cup water
¼	cup + 1 tablespoon apple juice
1	teaspoon vanilla

Topping

1	tablespoon kudzu
¾	cup apple juice
½	teaspoon grated lemon rind
½	teaspoon vanilla
1½	cups halved strawberries

TO MAKE THE COUSCOUS CAKE: In a large saucepan, combine the couscous, amazake, water, apple juice, and vanilla. Cook over medium heat, stirring constantly, for 10 minutes, or until the couscous starts swelling up. Transfer mixture to a baking dish. Spread with a spatula.

TO MAKE THE TOPPING: In a medium saucepan, combine the kudzu, apple juice, lemon rind, and vanilla. Cook on low heat until the kudzu dissolves and the sauce begins to thicken.

Arrange the strawberries evenly over the cake. Pour the kudzu mixture on top. Cool in the refrigerator before serving.

Makes 4 servings

Cooked Apples and Pears

½ cup raisins
4 cups water
2 apples, sliced
2 pears, sliced
¼ cup + 1–2 tablespoons kudzu
Water
Mint leaves

In a medium saucepan, combine the raisins and water. Bring to a boil over medium-high heat. Reduce the heat to medium and simmer for 8 to 10 minutes. Add the apples and pears. Cover and simmer for 15 minutes, or until the fruit turns soft. Reduce the heat to medium low.

In a small bowl, mix the kudzu with enough water to dissolve it. Add this to the fruit, stirring constantly to prevent lumps. Simmer on medium heat for 2 to 3 minutes, or until thickened. Serve warm in individual serving bowls. Garnish with mint.

Makes 2 servings

Variation: You can substitute other seasonal fruits, such as plums, apricots, or prunes, for the apples and pears.

Crunchy Stewed Plums

Stewed Plums

12	plums, halved and pitted
½	cup raisins
¾	cup + 2 tablespoons water
¼	cup maple syrup or barley malt
2	tablespoons kudzu
2	tablespoons water

Topping

1	cup rolled oats
4	tablespoons walnuts
4	tablespoons almonds
4	tablespoons sunflower seeds
2	tablespoons rice syrup

Preheat the oven to 350°F.

TO MAKE THE STEWED PLUMS: In a large saucepan, combine the plums, raisins, ¾ cup of the water, and the syrup or barley malt. Bring to a boil over medium heat. Cover and simmer on low for 5 to 8 minutes.

In a small bowl, dilute the kudzu in the remaining 2 tablespoons water. Mix until dissolved. Add to the plum mixture, stirring constantly. Simmer for 2 to 3 minutes. Pour into a baking dish and set aside.

TO MAKE THE TOPPING: In a medium skillet, cook the oats over medium-low heat until golden brown. Transfer into a small bowl. Add the walnuts, almonds, and sunflower seeds to the skillet. Cook lightly for 3 minutes. Add the rice syrup and stir to combine. Remove from the heat. Top the plums with the oats and syrup mixture. Serve warm.

Makes 2 servings

Carrot Macaroons

1	cup grated raw carrots
3	cups unsweetened shredded coconut
¾	cup whole-wheat flour
¼	cup water
½	cup maple syrup or honey
2	tablespoons sunflower oil
1	teaspoon almond extract
½	teaspoon vanilla

Preheat the oven to 350°F. Lightly coat a baking sheet with nonstick cooking spray.

In a medium bowl, mix together the carrots, coconut, and flour. Add the water, syrup or honey, oil, almond extract, and vanilla. Mix well. Allow to sit for 15 minutes.

Drop the batter onto the baking sheet in crescent shapes (like macaroons). Bake for 20 to 25 minutes, or until lightly browned.

Makes 12

Banana and Date Cookies

1½	bananas, mashed
2	cups chopped dates
2	cups rolled oats
1	cup chopped almonds
¼	cup oil
1	teaspoon vanilla

Preheat the oven to 350°F. Lightly coat a baking sheet with nonstick cooking spray.

(continued)

In a medium bowl, combine the bananas, dates, oats, almonds, oil, and vanilla. Mix well. Set aside for 10 minutes.

Roll the mixture into 1" balls and press flat on the baking sheet. Bake for 20 minutes, or until lightly browned.

Makes 24

FRUIT AND VEGETABLE JUICES

The best way to maximize the benefits of fresh juices is to incorporate them into your daily diet. Fresh fruit and vegetable juices are packed with natural vitamins, minerals, and other supplements, as opposed to the synthetic variety that come in pill form. The body does not need to make an effort to absorb these natural supplements, whereas the man-made variety still need to be broken down in order to penetrate the bloodstream.

By integrating the menus in this book with three 8-ounce glasses of fresh juice a day, you will experience a reduction in your blood toxicity levels and an improvement in your immune system. And you'll see the results within the first two weeks of this healthy regimen. If you want to restore your health and maintain a simple and effective—yet not drastic—regimen, try drinking at least one glass of fresh juice every day, and over the course of several weeks or months, switch from your normal diet to meals created from our recipes. This will progressively build up your health.

It's best to drink fresh juices in the morning on an empty stomach, as all the health properties in the juice will be easily absorbed into your bloodstream and you will obtain the maximum benefit. (Be aware, however, that the acidity of orange juice troubles some people when they drink it on an empty stomach.) You can follow with a fruit breakfast from our breakfast menus. If you eat toast, croissants, or bread with your juice, they will soak up the juice in your stomach and you may feel bloated. If possible, allow for a 20-minute time lapse between one item and the other, or try eating a bowl of cereal with nondairy milk instead.

Drink fresh juices all day long; they make great energy-boosters after a workout or in mid to late afternoon, when your energy levels sink during a day of hard work. They are also very good when you are feeling ill and not very hungry, since they provide the essential nutrients without overworking your digestive system. In this case, serve them freshly made and at room temperature, not chilled, so they're gentler to your system.

There are infinite combinations of fruit and vegetable juices. Explore your own juice combinations and make up "cocktails," choosing seasonal fruits and vegetables. The following juices can be made in a juicer; the quantities listed will make one serving, unless otherwise indicated.

Carrot and Celery Juice

5 carrots, with ends removed

4 stalks celery

Carrot is the king of all vegetable juices. It contains provitamin A (which the body converts into vitamin A); vitamins B, C, D, E, and K, and the minerals calcium, phosphorus, potassium, sodium, and trace minerals. It cleanses the lining of the colon and the intestines and it is one of the most naturally perfect cleansers and tonics for the liver. Through regular use, carrot juice helps the liver release excess bile and stale fats. When fat levels are reduced, cholesterol is also reduced.

Celery has a calming effect on the nervous system and is a rich source of organic sodium (natural salt), which is less harmful than inorganic table salt because it naturally combines with many other minerals—the salty taste of our blood is due to it being high in organic sodium. In weight-reduction diets, celery juice helps reduce cravings for sweets.

Watermelon Juice

Juice the entire fruit

Juicing the rind, seeds, and pulp of the watermelon makes the juice sweeter and adds many minerals contained in the rind. This is a great kidney and bladder cleanser. It also helps regulate excess fluids in the body, stimulates the appetite, and contains plenty of enzymes. On hot summer days, drink it very cold throughout the day. One small watermelon will make several glasses.

Apple and Pineapple Juice

⅙ *pineapple, skinned*
2–3 firm apples, of any variety (not waxed)

Pineapple juice is sweet, thirst-quenching, and very delicious when combined with apples. It is rich in vitamin C, enzymes, and fruit acids, and it soothes sore throats. It also contains bromelain, which helps neutralize foods that are too alkaline or too acidic and thus helps with indigestion.

Apple juice is rich in vitamins A, B_1, B_2, B_6, and C, biotin, folic acid, pantothenic acid, and the minerals chlorine, copper, iron, magnesium, manganese, phosphorus, potassium, silicon, sodium, and sulfur. The fresh vitamin C in apple juice helps prevent colds, flu, and intestinal infections. Its high pectin content also makes it an excellent natural bowel regulator.

Beet, Carrot, and Celery Juice

1½ *uncooked beets, peeled*
5–6 carrots
3–4 stalks celery

Beet juice is an excellent source of vitamin B_6, choline, organic sodium, potassium, and natural sugars. Beets yield high-quality iron that helps build red blood cells and is easily and effectively absorbed into the bloodstream. This is an excellent juice for winter, when we need to build strength and keep our blood fluid to maintain good circulation. It is also very good for people with anemia and for women to drink during menstruation. Beets are powerful kidney cleansers, so it's a good idea to start by using a juice mixture of ¼ beet to ¾ carrot and celery and build up slowly to ½ beet to ½ carrot and celery. This is a powerful cocktail.

Orange and Grapefruit Juice

1½ *oranges*
1½ *grapefruits, peeled, seeded, and quartered (pink and red ones are sweeter and less acidic than white ones)*

This combination makes a powerful tonic and cleanser for the gastrointestinal tract. It also improves and strengthens capillary walls, benefiting the heart and lungs. Orange juice contains large amounts of vitamins A and C as well as minerals, bioflavonoids, amino acids, and folic acid.

Grapefruit juice is also a rich source of vitamin C. This combination is excellent for treating common colds and sore throats. Grapefruit juice, for instance, will produce a light sweat and relieve fever.

Pineapple, Apple, Pear, Strawberry,
and Raspberry Juice

⅙ *pineapple*
1½ *apples, of any variety (not waxed)*
1 *pear*
6–8 *strawberries*
5–6 *raspberries*

This is a delicious fruit cocktail packed with vitamins. The pear makes for a thicker consistency, so that it resembles a smoothie more than a liquid juice. This is the perfect drink for late spring and early summer.

NONDAIRY SMOOTHIES

Fruit smoothies are highly nutritious and healthy substitute beverages for the midmorning and afternoon coffee or tea rituals. Drink them in all seasons. If at lunchtime you are not feeling overly hungry or are short of time, you can drink a smoothie since they are packed with all the necessary vitamins and nutrients. They are also great after a workout. It's best to drink smoothies on their own, apart from foods, as they represent complete meals in themselves.

Below are some tips to keep in mind when making fruit smoothies using the recipes that follow.

- Frozen bananas provide the creamy texture to all nondairy fruit smoothies. To freeze, place unpeeled bananas in the freezer overnight.

- Use natural sweeteners such as honey, organic maple syrup, or dates.

- If you have difficulty digesting frozen fruits, use fruits at room temperature and combine in the blender with fruit juices that have been frozen beforehand.

- Use fresh or shredded coconut to add creamy texture to smoothies.

Banana, Date, and Apple Smoothie

    2   bananas, frozen
        Juice of 1½ apples, frozen
    6   dates
        Soy milk (optional)

Thaw the bananas and apple juice for 30 minutes.

In a blender or food processor, combine the bananas, apple juice, and dates. Blend thoroughly on high speed. To dilute, use more apple juice or a little soy milk.

Makes 1 serving

Pineapple, Banana, and Strawberry Smoothie

        Juice of ⅙ pineapple, frozen
    2   bananas, frozen
    6–7 strawberries, frozen

Thaw the pineapple juice, bananas, and strawberries for 30 minutes.

In a blender or food processor, combine the pineapple juice, bananas, and strawberries. Blend thoroughly.

Makes 1 serving

Papaya, Banana, and Coconut Smoothie

    ½   papaya, frozen
    2   bananas, frozen
    1   glass coconut milk, frozen

Thaw the papaya, bananas, and coconut milk for 30 minutes.

In a blender or food processor, combine the papaya, bananas, and coconut milk. Blend thoroughly.

Makes 1 serving

Banana-Blueberry Smoothie with Maple Syrup

2	bananas, frozen
10–15	blueberries, frozen
3	tablespoons maple syrup

Thaw the bananas and blueberries for 30 minutes.

In a blender or food processor, combine the bananas, blueberries, and syrup. Blend thoroughly.

Makes 1 serving

Watermelon and Cantaloupe Smoothie

Pulp of ½ watermelon, seeded, cut into 1" cubes, and frozen
Juice of ½ watermelon, frozen
Pulp of ½ cantaloupe, cut into 1" cubes and frozen

Thaw the watermelon pulp, watermelon juice, and cantaloupe for 30 minutes.

In a blender or food processor, combine the watermelon pulp, watermelon juice, and cantaloupe. Blend thoroughly.

Makes 4 servings

Chapter 5

SPRING

HE EQUINOX ON MARCH 21 marks the beginning of spring, the
season of blossoms. For the next six months, yang energy progressively
grows and is dominant in nature—everything is being born again. There is
a marked increase in the amount of sunlight during the days, awakening us
from the sleep of winter. This is the perfect time for long walks in nature,
where the sight of the green plants growing heals our bodies and nourishes our souls. Outdoor activities also help us to oxygenate after the long
winter months, and our appetites decrease and we get rid of winter fat.

This is a time for fresh beginnings, new resolutions, and looking at life
and its mysteries with new, cleansed eyes. Chinese medicine says that spring
strips off the invisible membrane over our eyes and minds, giving us a clearer picture. Now is the time to use positive energy to change old, destructive patterns, to renew friendships, and to remember all those relationships
and activities that bring us joy, wholeness, and fulfillment.

To keep pace with this new brighter and lighter phase, we eat foods
that promote the taste for this season—sour. This is the season in which we

eat less or even fast to cleanse our bodies of the excesses of autumn and winter, and we pay special attention to the liver and gallbladder.

Spring cooking methods: Steaming raw food and quick cooking at high temperatures, such as stir-frying.

Spring vegetables: Green beans, peppers, many types of young plants, new potatoes, baby asparagus, sprouts, cereal grasses (wheat), young beets, carrots, starchy vegetables, lemons, and leafy greens.

Spring grains: Quinoa, barley, rye, oats, and sprouted grains.

Spring fruits: Apples and pears.

Special spring foods: Emphasize fermented foods like tempeh, sauerkraut, and live-culture yogurt.

Spring herbs: Basil, caraway, parsley, dill, and bay leaf; also raw onion and garlic to help with digestion.

Suggested spring body therapies: All therapies in spring should be aimed at cleansing and renewal—long walks in nature, in forests, and by water to oxygenate the lungs. Also open-air activities such as gardening or tai chi in the park. To help cleansing, eat raw food and drink fresh juices.

Suggested spring diet: Salads, sushi, lightly steamed vegetables, stir-fries, sandwiches, light seasonings. Use less oil in your meals and moderate the use of vinegar and lemons.

LUNCH

Tempeh Sandwiches

¼	cup sunflower oil
1	clove garlic, chopped
3	thin slices tempeh
2	tablespoons tamari
6	slices rye bread
¾	cup Tofu Russian Dressing (see page 82)

(continued)

¾ cup watercress or alfalfa sprouts
   Chopped onions or scallions
1 medium tomato, thinly sliced

In a medium skillet, heat the oil over medium-high heat. Reduce the heat to medium and add the garlic and tempeh. Cook, turning the tempeh occasionally, until it is browned on both sides. Add the tamari and cook until heated.

Lightly toast the bread and spread 3 slices with the Russian dressing. Place an equal amount of watercress or sprouts on each slice. Top each with a slice of tempeh, the onions or scallions, tomatoes, and another slice of toast. Serve immediately or wrap well and refrigerate.

Makes 3

Lentil Burgers

2   cups green lentils, rinsed and drained
3¾   cups vegetable stock
1   bay leaf
     Pinch of sea salt
     Pinch of ground black pepper
¼   cup extra-virgin olive oil
1   onion, chopped
1   clove garlic, chopped
1½   cups mushrooms, finely chopped
2   tablespoons tomato puree
     Finely chopped fresh parsley
½   cup dry bread crumbs
¼   cup whole-wheat flour seasoned with 1 tablespoon fine
     herbs or dried Italian seasoning
     Tomato slices
     Cucumber slices

In a large saucepan, combine the lentils, stock, bay leaf, salt, and pepper. Cover and simmer over medium heat for 45 minutes to 1 hour, or until the lentils are tender. Remove from the heat.

In a colander, drain the lentils. Remove and discard the bay leaf. Transfer the lentils to a large bowl and mash coarsely with a potato masher. Set aside.

In a medium skillet over medium-high heat, heat 2 tablespoons of the oil. Add the onions and garlic. Cook until lightly browned. Add the mushrooms and cook, stirring, for 2 to 4 minutes, or until the mushrooms release their liquid.

Add the mushroom mixture, tomato puree, parsley, and bread crumbs to the lentils. Stir to combine. Transfer to a medium bowl and set aside.

With your hands, form the mixture into 2 patties. Place them on a platter and set aside for 30 minutes.

On a plate or in a shallow bowl, dredge the burgers in the flour. In a medium skillet over medium-high heat, heat the remaining 2 tablespoons oil. Add the burgers and cook, turning, until browned on both sides. Serve with the tomato and cucumber slices and your favorite savory dip.

Makes 2

Variation: For a low-fat alternative, the burgers can be grilled.

Barley and Hazelnut Salad

Vinaigrette

2	tablespoons hazelnut oil
4	teaspoons lemon juice
1	teaspoon wine vinegar
2	scallions, finely chopped
1	clove garlic, chopped
2	tablespoons orange juice

Salad

1¼	cups barley, rinsed
3	cups vegetable stock

(continued)

¼	cup olive oil
¾	cup finely chopped celery
1	cup finely chopped carrots
1½	cups hazelnuts, finely chopped
¼	cup chopped fresh parsley
¼	cup currants, soaked in hot water and drained
	Pinch of sea salt
	Pinch of ground black pepper
1	cup toasted hazelnuts

To make the vinaigrette: In a small bowl, whisk together the oil, lemon juice, vinegar, scallions, garlic, and orange juice.

To make the salad: In a large saucepan, bring the barley and stock to a boil over medium-high heat. Reduce the heat to medium and simmer until the stock is absorbed. Remove from the heat and set aside to cool.

Transfer to a medium bowl and add the oil, celery, carrots, nuts, parsley, and currants.

Toss the salad with the vinaigrette. Season with the salt and pepper and sprinkle with the nuts.

Makes 2 main-course or 4 side-dish servings

Baked Tofu and Curly Endive Salad

Baked Tofu

3	cloves garlic, chopped
2	tablespoons tomato puree
4	teaspoons wine vinegar
3	tablespoons tamari
2	tablespoons water
1	block tofu (8 ounces), drained and cut into 1" pieces
¼	cup dry bread crumbs or corn flour

Salad

2   tablespoons sesame oil
1   medium red onion, sliced
    Pinch of dried oregano
2   cups mushrooms, sliced
1   clove garlic, chopped
3   teaspoons black sesame seeds, toasted
1   bunch curly endive

To make the baked tofu: Preheat the broiler. In a medium bowl, whisk together the garlic, tomato puree, vinegar, tamari, and water. Add the tofu and toss to combine. Cover and refrigerate for 30 minutes, tossing once or twice.

In a medium bowl, add the drained tofu to the bread crumbs or corn flour and stir to coat. Place on a broiler pan under medium heat and broil for 12 minutes, turning over after 6 minutes to brown both sides.

To make the salad: In a medium skillet over medium-high heat, heat 1½ tablespoons of the oil. Reduce the heat to medium. Add the onions and oregano. Cook until softened. Add the mushrooms and garlic. Cook, stirring, until the mushrooms soften and release their liquid. Sprinkle with the sesame seeds.

Wash the endive and place in a large bowl. Sprinkle with the remaining ½ tablespoon oil.

Add the tofu to the mushrooms and toss. Serve over the endive.

Makes 2 main-course or 4 side-dish servings

Butter Bean Bruschetta with Garlic Mustard Greens

2½   tablespoons olive oil
1   small onion, chopped
½   teaspoon dried thyme

(continued)

½   teaspoon dried sage
½   teaspoon sea salt
1   stalk celery, chopped
2   cloves garlic, chopped
1½ cups cooked butter beans
1   tablespoon tomato puree
1   teaspoon cider vinegar
2   cups chopped steamed mustard greens
    Pinch of ground black pepper
1   large tomato, chopped
4   slices (1½" thick) Italian bread

In a medium skillet over medium heat, heat 1 tablespoon of the oil. Add the onions, thyme, sage, and ¼ teaspoon of the salt. Cook until the onions begin to soften. Add the celery and half of the garlic. Cook until transparent.

Add the beans, tomato puree, and vinegar. Cook, stirring, until the beans are heated through, crushing them with the back of a wooden spoon as they cook. Transfer the beans to a blender or food processor and blend until smooth. Drizzle with ½ tablespoon of the oil.

In another medium skillet over medium heat, heat the remaining 1 tablespoon oil, the remaining garlic, and the greens. Stir to coat evenly with oil. Sprinkle with the remaining ¼ teaspoon salt, the pepper, and tomatoes. Set aside.

Toast the bread lightly. Mound the bean puree on the bread and top with the greens.

Makes 4 side-dish servings

DINNER

STARTERS

Spinach and Chickpea Soup with Cumin Croutons

Soup

3	tablespoons extra-virgin olive oil
1	red onion, diced
3	cloves garlic, chopped
	Pinch of sea salt
	Pinch of ground black pepper
1	teaspoon ground cumin
¼	teaspoon ground nutmeg
1	bay leaf
2	cloves
1½	cups cooked chickpeas
4	cups Curry Stock (see page 89)
4	cups chopped spinach
1	tablespoon lemon juice

Croutons

1	egg white
1	teaspoon chopped garlic
2	teaspoons ground cumin
½	teaspoon sea salt
2	teaspoons chopped cilantro
1½	cups small bread cubes

To make the soup: In a soup pot over medium heat, warm the oil. Add the onions, garlic, salt, and pepper, and cook for 3 minutes, or until the onions begin to soften.

Add the cumin, nutmeg, bay leaf, and cloves. Cook, stirring, for 2 minutes. (If the mixture seems too dry, add a little water.)

Add the chickpeas and 2 cups of the stock. Simmer for 10 minutes. Add the spinach and cook until wilted. Add the remaining 2 cups stock, bring to a boil, and simmer for 10 to 15 minutes. Let the soup cool slightly. Remove and discard the bay leaf and cloves.

In a blender or food processor, blend until pureed. Return the soup to the pot and season with the lemon juice. If necessary, thin the soup with water.

To make the croutons: Preheat the oven to 350°F. Coat a baking sheet with nonstick cooking spray.

In a medium bowl, beat the egg white until frothy. Add the garlic, cumin, salt, and cilantro. Stir to combine. Add the bread cubes and toss to coat. Place on the prepared baking sheet and bake for 10 minutes, or until lightly browned.

Add the croutons to the soup and serve.

Makes 4 servings

Stuffed Zucchini with Olive and Tomato Sauce

Stuffed Zucchini

3	medium zucchini, washed and halved lengthwise
1	sprig thyme
3	tablespoons extra-virgin olive oil

1   large onion, chopped
2   cloves garlic, chopped
    Pinch of sea salt
1   tablespoon chopped fresh basil
1   tablespoon chopped fresh parsley
2   firm tomatoes, peeled, seeded, and chopped
¼   cup whole-wheat dry bread crumbs
¼   cup ground walnuts

Sauce

¼   cup olive paste
¼   cup tomato puree
1   tablespoon water

Preheat the oven to 350°F. Coat a large baking sheet with nonstick cooking spray.

To make the stuffed zucchini: Preheat the broiler. With a spoon, remove the zucchini pulp. Chop the pulp and set aside.

On a steaming rack over a large pot of salted, boiling water, steam the zucchini halves and thyme for 6 to 8 minutes, or until soft but not mushy. Transfer to the prepared baking sheet and let cool.

Meanwhile, in a medium skillet over medium-high heat, heat 2 tablespoons of the oil. Reduce the heat to medium. Add the onions, garlic, and salt. Cook, stirring, until lightly browned. Add the basil, parsley, and the zucchini pulp. Mix well and cook for 2 minutes. Add the tomatoes and cook until heated through. Remove from the heat, and add the bread crumbs and nuts. Stir to combine.

Spoon the stuffing into the zucchini halves and drizzle with the remaining 1 tablespoon oil.

Bake for 15 to 20 minutes, then place under the broiler to brown the tops.

(continued)

TO MAKE THE SAUCE: In a small saucepan, combine the olive paste, tomato puree, and water. Warm the sauce slightly over medium heat. Spoon over the stuffed zucchini and serve warm.

Makes 6 servings

Asparagus Oriental-Style

Sauce

2	teaspoons cornstarch
1	tablespoon water
2	tablespoons tamari
½	teaspoon honey
1	tablespoon sherry
1	tablespoon sesame oil

Asparagus

1¼	pounds asparagus
2	teaspoons sesame oil
1	leek, julienned
2	cloves garlic, chopped
1	tablespoon minced fresh ginger
¼	cup water
	Toasted sesame seeds

TO MAKE THE SAUCE: In a medium bowl, mix the cornstarch and water. Add the tamari, honey, sherry, and oil. Stir to combine. Set aside.

TO MAKE THE ASPARAGUS: Rinse the asparagus and remove the tough ends. In a wok, heat the oil over medium–high heat. Add the leeks and cook for 2 minutes. Add the garlic and ginger. Cook and stir for a few seconds. Add the asparagus and stir, then add the water. Simmer for 5 minutes, or until the vegetables are tender.

Whisk the sauce and pour it over the vegetables. Raise the heat to high. Cook and stir for 1 minute, or until the sauce thickens.

Serve warm, with a sprinkling of sesame seeds.

Makes 4 servings

Cauliflower Soufflé

Soufflé

2	tablespoons dry bread crumbs
4	slices whole-wheat bread
	Soy milk
1	large head cauliflower
2	tablespoons olive oil
1	clove garlic, chopped
1	teaspoon chopped fresh herbs
	Pinch of sea salt
	Pinch of ground black pepper
1	teaspoon prepared mustard

Sauce

¾	cup vegetable stock
1	cup fresh parsley, finely chopped
¼	cup walnuts, chopped and toasted
¼	cup soy cream or soy milk

TO MAKE THE SOUFFLÉ: Preheat the oven to 350°F. Liberally coat a soufflé pan with nonstick cooking spray and sprinkle with the bread crumbs.

Place the bread slices in a shallow dish with enough milk to cover. Set aside to soak for 15 minutes.

(continued)

Trim the cauliflower and cut into large pieces. On a steaming rack over a large pot of boiling water, steam for 20 to 30 minutes. Break the cauliflower into small pieces.

In a wok, heat the oil over medium-high heat. Add the cauliflower and stir well to coat.

In a blender or food processor, blend the soaked bread and cauliflower until pureed. Return the mixture to the wok and add the garlic, herbs, salt, pepper, and mustard. Cook until heated through.

Pour the cauliflower puree into the prepared pan and bake for 15 minutes, or until the top browns.

TO MAKE THE SAUCE: In a medium saucepan, heat the stock, parsley, and nuts over medium heat. When hot, stir in the soy cream or soy milk. Serve over the soufflé.

Makes 4 servings

Artichoke Crostini

1	baguette, cut into 8 (1" thick) slices
3	tablespoons olive oil
¼	cup black olive paste
2	small cloves garlic, mashed
1	small tomato, thinly sliced
8	marinated artichokes, cut lengthwise into quarters

Preheat the broiler. Arrange the baguette slices on a baking sheet and, using 2 tablespoons of the oil, brush both sides of each slice. Toast under the broiler until lightly browned.

In a medium bowl, combine the olive paste, garlic, and about ½ tablespoon oil. Spread an equal amount of paste on each slice. Top each slice with tomatoes and artichokes. Drizzle with the remaining ½ tablespoon oil. Place under the broiler briefly to heat through, and serve.

Makes 8 servings

ENTRÉES

Tofu-and-Vegetable Kabobs with Saffron-Cardamom Rice

Marinade

3	tablespoons soy sauce
1	tablespoon tomato paste
2	cloves garlic, crushed
1	tablespoon sugar
1	teaspoon vinegar
¼	cup olive oil

Kabobs

1	green pepper, cut into large pieces
1	sweet yellow pepper, cut into large pieces
8	shallots, peeled
8	baby squash or zucchini
1½	cups drained, pressed, cubed tofu (about 12 pieces)
8	mushrooms

Rice

1¼	cups basmati rice
1	tablespoon sunflower oil
2	whole cardamom pods, crushed
1	cinnamon stick
2¼	cups water
	Pinch of sea salt
¼	teaspoon saffron threads dissolved in 2 tablespoons warm water
1	tablespoon golden raisins, soaked in hot water and drained

To make the marinade: In a small bowl, combine the soy sauce, tomato paste, garlic, sugar, vinegar, and oil. Set aside.

To make the kabobs: Preheat the broiler. Thread the green and yellow peppers, shallots, squash or zucchini, and tofu onto 4 bamboo skewers that have been soaked in water. Brush on all sides with the marinade and place in a deep baking dish. Pour the remaining marinade over the kabobs. Marinate for 4 to 6 hours.

Place the kabobs on a broiler pan and brush with the marinade. Broil for 5 to 7 minutes, turning occasionally and brushing with marinade.

To make the rice: Wash the rice in several changes of water. Place in a medium bowl with water to cover and let soak for 30 minutes.

In a medium saucepan, heat the oil over medium-high heat. Add the cardamom and cinnamon. Cook for 1 to 2 minutes.

Drain the rice and add it to the pan. Reduce the heat to low and cook for 3 minutes. Add the water and salt. Raise the heat to medium-high and bring to a boil. Reduce the heat to medium and simmer until the water is absorbed.

Stir in the dissolved saffron and the raisins just before serving, and fluff with a fork. Remove and discard the cinnamon stick.

Makes 4 servings

Note: If necessary, the rice can be kept warm in a 325°F oven.

Pasta Primavera

3	sweet red peppers
¼	cup extra-virgin olive oil
1	red onion, sliced
2	cloves garlic, chopped
2	leeks, finely chopped
2½	cups Swiss chard, cut into strips
2	cups peas
	Pinch of sea salt

Pinch of ground black pepper
6 tablespoons chopped scallions
½ teaspoon five-spice powder
1 pound soba noodles, tagliatelle, or spinach fettuccine
2 tablespoons pine nuts, toasted
6–8 fresh basil leaves, cut into strips

Preheat the broiler. In a large broiling pan, broil the red peppers about 4" from the heat for about 3 minutes, turning them so that all sides are evenly charred. Place the peppers in a covered container for about 5 minutes. The moisture that is released by their heat will make the skins easier to remove. Using a paring knife, peel the skins off and remove the seeds and ribs.

In a blender or food processor, puree the peppers.

In a medium skillet, heat the oil over medium-high heat. Reduce the heat to medium. Add the onions, garlic, leeks, Swiss chard, peas, salt, and black pepper. Stir-fry until the vegetables are softened.

Add the pepper puree, scallions, and five-spice powder to the skillet. Cook until heated through.

Cook the pasta according to the package directions. Drain. In a large bowl, toss the pasta with the vegetable sauce. Sprinkle with the pine nuts and basil.

Makes 4 servings

Spicy Black Bean Stew with Apple Polenta

Black Bean Stew

1½ cups black beans, soaked overnight
3½ cups water
½ teaspoon sea salt

(continued)

1	bay leaf
2	tablespoons olive oil
3	teaspoons cumin seeds
1	teaspoon chopped fresh basil
1	teaspoon chopped fresh oregano
2	medium onions, chopped
3	cloves garlic, chopped
2	stalks celery, chopped
1½	teaspoons ground coriander
	Pinch of ground paprika
1	carrot, diced
1	medium sweet yellow pepper, chopped
1½	cups peeled, seeded, and chopped tomatoes
1	tablespoon rice vinegar
¼	cup chopped fresh cilantro
	Pinch of ground black pepper

Rinse and drain the beans. Place in a medium saucepan with the water, ¼ teaspoon of the salt, and the bay leaf. Bring to a boil over medium–high heat. Reduce the heat to medium, cover, and simmer for 1½ hours, or until tender. When the beans are cooked, drain them in a colander. Reserve the cooking liquid.

In a large skillet over medium heat, heat 1 tablespoon of the oil. Add the cumin seeds, and when they begin to color, add the basil and oregano. Stir frequently to keep the herbs from scorching, adding extra oil, if necessary.

Add the onions, garlic, celery, coriander, paprika, and the remaining ¼ teaspoon salt. Cook for 15 minutes. Add the carrots and yellow peppers. Mix well and cook for about 5 minutes. Add the tomatoes, stir, and simmer for 10 to 12 minutes. (If the mixture looks dry, add some of the reserved cooking liquid.)

Add the beans to the tomato mixture and cook for 30 minutes, or until the beans are tender and the mixture is heated through. (If it looks dry, add some of the reserved cooking liquid.)

Sprinkle with the vinegar, cilantro, and black pepper.

Makes 4 servings

Grilled Polenta with Apple and Raisin Sauce

Polenta

4 cups water
1 teaspoon sea salt
1 teaspoon ground black pepper
2½ cups coarse cornmeal
2 tablespoons extra-virgin olive oil

Sauce

¾ cup warm apple cider
2½ cups peeled and diced green apples
2 tablespoons maple syrup
¾ cup raisins, soaked in hot water and drained
½ teaspoon ground allspice
½ teaspoon ground cinnamon
1 teaspoon sea salt
1 teaspoon ground red pepper

To make the polenta: Coat a 5" × 9" glass baking dish with nonstick cooking spray. Preheat the broiler. In a large saucepan or double boiler, bring the water to a boil over medium-high heat. Add the salt and pepper. Add the cornmeal in a thin stream, stirring constantly with a wooden spoon to avoid lumps. Reduce the heat to medium and cook, stirring constantly, for 30 minutes. (If using a double boiler, cook for 45 minutes.)

Pour the cooked polenta into the prepared baking dish. Set aside for 5 to 10 minutes to cool and set. Cut into ½" slices, place on a broiler pan, and brush with the oil. Broil until browned.

To make the sauce: In a large saucepan, combine the cider, apples, and maple syrup. Cook over medium heat for 8 to 10 minutes, or until

(continued)

the apples are tender. Stir in the raisins, allspice, cinnamon, salt, and pepper. Cook for 2 minutes, or until heated through. Serve with the polenta.

Makes 4 servings

Sushi with Beans and Gingered Tofu

Vegetarian Sushi

1¼	cups white rice
2	cups water
2	tablespoons rice vinegar
¼	cup mirin
½	teaspoon sea salt
1	medium cucumber, peeled and halved lengthwise
4	sheets nori, toasted
1	tablespoon wasabi, dissolved in water
	Pickled ginger
	Tamari

In a large sieve, rinse the rice until the water runs clear.

In a medium saucepan, combine the rice and water. Cover and cook over medium heat for 10 to 12 minutes. Reduce the heat to low and cook until the water is fully absorbed. Remove from the heat and let stand, covered, for 10 minutes.

In a small saucepan, heat the vinegar, mirin, and salt over low heat until the salt is dissolved. Transfer the rice to a large bowl and fan vigorously to cool it. Slowly stir in the vinegar mixture. Continue fanning and stirring until cool.

With a spoon, scoop the seeds from the cucumber and cut into ½" strips. Place a sheet of nori on a bamboo rolling mat, and with damp hands, cover it with a layer of rice. Spread a thin line of wasabi across the rice from left to right. Using a bamboo roller, place a ½" line of cucumber strips over the wasabi. Roll the sushi away from you, and using a sharp, wet knife, cut into 1" pieces. Serve with the ginger and tamari.

Makes 4 servings

Green Bean Salad

3 cups water
3 cups green beans, stringed and cut into 2" pieces
¼ cup miso
  Toasted sesame seeds
1 tablespoon mirin
1 tablespoon sugar

In a large saucepan, bring the water to a boil over medium-high heat. Reduce the heat to medium, add the beans, cover, and cook until tender. In a colander, rinse the beans with cold water. Transfer to a medium bowl and set aside.

In a small bowl, combine the miso, sesame seeds, mirin, and sugar.

Add the dressing to the cooked beans and stir to coat. Let stand for 15 minutes before serving.

Makes 4 servings

Ginger Tofu

1¼ cups drained, pressed, cubed tofu
¼ cup corn flour
2 tablespoons vegetable oil
2 leeks, washed and sliced
1 piece (1") fresh ginger, julienned
¼ cup tamari

(continued)

1	tablespoon mirin
1	tablespoon sugar
1	cup water
4	scallions, sliced diagonally
½	cup bean sprouts

Dust the tofu with the flour.

In a medium skillet, heat 1 tablespoon of the oil over medium-high heat. Reduce the heat to medium, add the tofu, and cook, stirring often, until browned. Remove from the pan and drain on a paper towel.

In the skillet, heat the remaining 1 tablespoon oil. Add the leeks and ginger. Cook for 2 to 3 minutes. Add the tamari, mirin, sugar, and water. Cook, stirring, for 3 to 4 minutes.

Return the tofu to the skillet and cook, stirring, for 2 to 3 minutes. Serve hot, sprinkled with the scallions and bean sprouts.

Makes 4 servings

Mediterranean Casserole and Greek Salad

Mediterranean Casserole

Casserole

2	tablespoons sunflower oil
2	onions, sliced
2	cloves garlic, crushed
4	zucchini, sliced and salted
4	tomatoes, sliced
	Pinch of sea salt
	Pinch of ground black pepper
2	tablespoons chopped fresh basil
¼	cup vegetable stock

1   tablespoon tomato puree
1   teaspoon pesto

Topping

3   tablespoons dry bread crumbs
2   tablespoons fresh chopped parsley
2   tablespoons chopped celery
2   tablespoons chopped onions

Preheat the oven to 350°F. Oil a 9" round or square baking dish.

TO MAKE THE CASSEROLE: In a medium skillet, heat the oil over medium-high heat. Reduce the heat to medium and add the onions and garlic. Cook until slightly softened.

In the prepared baking dish, place a layer of zucchini, then a layer of onions, and finally a layer of tomatoes. Repeat until you have 3 layers, finishing with the tomatoes. Sprinkle with the salt, pepper, and basil.

In a medium bowl, combine the stock, tomato puree, and pesto. Pour evenly over the casserole. Cover with foil and bake for 45 minutes.

TO MAKE THE TOPPING: In a medium bowl, combine the bread crumbs, parsley, celery, and onions. Remove the foil from the casserole and spread the bread crumb mixture on top. Place under the broiler for 5 minutes, or until the top is browned. Serve hot or at room temperature.

Makes 4 servings

Greek Salad

1   head romaine lettuce, washed and torn into bite-size
    pieces
    Baby spinach or arugula
    Greek olives
1   sweet red pepper, cut into thin strips
1   sweet yellow pepper, cut into thin strips
1   red onion, thinly sliced

(continued)

Sun-dried tomatoes, chopped
½ avocado, thinly sliced
½ cucumber, thinly sliced
1 stalk celery, thinly sliced
Feta cheese or tofu cubes or bread croutons

In a large salad bowl, combine the lettuce, spinach or arugula, olives, red peppers, yellow peppers, onions, tomatoes, avocado, cucumbers, celery, and the cheese, tofu, or croutons. Toss well with the dressing of your choice.

Makes 4 servings

Chapter 6

MIDSUMMER

I N SUMMER, YANG ENERGY is at its height in nature—everything is ripening and bearing fruit. To unify with this beautiful season we will express expansion, growth, lightness, outward activity, and creativity. June 21 sets the beginning of summer, when days are longer and nights shorter. This is the time for outdoor activities, like swimming at the seashore or in lakes, with long hours spent in contact with nature, wearing little clothing so as to expose the skin to the warm rays of the sun.

A symphony of colors surrounds us, and our summer tables should carry these colors through with dazzling displays of the abundant produce available now. This is the time for informal eating and great get-togethers with family and friends—picnics, outdoor barbecues, eating in the garden or on the patio.

In summer, we must pay particular attention to balancing our meals with the heat. To counteract the heat, eat plenty of cooling foods at room temperature (icy cold drinks and ice creams can contract the digestive system), drink plenty of liquids, and try eating when the sun is not at its hottest (lunch should be later than normal and dinner should be well after sunset). Try to create a cool atmosphere in your house by closing shutters early in the morning to trap the fresh air, using light cotton sheets on beds, and watering your plants and garden frequently before and after the sun is at its fullest intensity.

Summer cooking methods: Raw foods, light steaming, and cooking at high heats for short times, such as stir-frying.

Summer vegetables: Lettuce, endive, watercress, cucumbers, cabbage, alfalfa, corn, mushrooms, bean sprouts, scallions, and green, leafy bitter vegetables.

Summer grains: Rolled oats, lentils, millet, and yellow corn.

Summer fruits: Strawberries, apricots, cherries, red plums, and peaches.

Summer drinks: Preferably at room temperature—lemonade, occasionally sprinkled with ginger; iced teas, especially fruity ones such as strawberry tea; and fruit and vegetable juices.

Summer herbs: Mint, chrysanthemum, and horseradish.

Suggested summer body therapies: Swimming, scuba diving, jogging, tennis and outdoor ball games, color therapy, outdoor yoga, and tai chi.

Suggested summer diet: Very light meals, preferably taken often in small quantities, emphasizing lunch as the main meal. Crisp salads, cold udon noodles with tofu, corn on the cob, raw vegetables with a dressing, and fruit salads.

LUNCH

Easy Tofu Burgers

Good toppings for these burgers include tomatoes, alfalfa sprouts, dill pickles, cucumbers, and soy mayonnaise.

>1 tablespoon extra-virgin olive oil
>½ cup chopped scallions

2 cups grated cabbage
2 cups shredded carrots
1 cup drained, crumbled firm tofu
2 tablespoons soy sauce
2 teaspoons baking powder
1 teaspoon dried oregano
½ teaspoon paprika
½ teaspoon ground ginger
¾ cup whole-wheat flour
4 whole-wheat buns

Preheat the oven to 325°F. Oil a large baking sheet.

In a medium skillet, warm the oil over medium heat. Add the scallions, cabbage, and carrots. Sauté, stirring constantly, for 4 to 5 minutes, or until slightly tender. Remove from the heat. Transfer the vegetables to a medium bowl.

In a blender or food processor, cream the tofu. Add the soy sauce, baking powder, oregano, paprika, and ginger. Blend well. Add the tofu mixture to the bowl and mix well with the vegetables.

Using your hands, mold the mixture into flat patties and coat them with flour. Place the patties on the baking sheet. Bake for 15 minutes. Turn over and bake for 10 minutes more, or until lightly browned. Serve on the buns with toppings of your choice.

Makes 4

Variation: The burgers can also be cooked on a grill until brown.

Salad of Broiled Summer Vegetables

1 large onion, sliced
1 large zucchini, sliced diagonally 1" thick
2 large yellow squash, sliced diagonally 1" thick
2 large carrots, sliced diagonally ¼" thick

(continued)

1   large sweet red pepper, cut into squares
1   large green pepper, cut into squares
¼   cup + 2 tablespoons extra-virgin olive oil
2   tablespoons balsamic vinegar
    Pinch of sea salt
    Pinch of ground black pepper
1   tablespoon chopped fresh basil
1   tablespoon chopped fresh parsley

Preheat the broiler. Coat a large baking sheet with nonstick cooking spray.

In a large bowl, combine the onions, zucchini, squash, carrots, red peppers, and green peppers. Add ¼ cup of the oil, the vinegar, salt, pepper, and three-fourths of the basil and parsley. Toss well, so the oil coats the vegetables evenly.

Transfer to the baking sheet and broil about 4" from the heat for about 5 minutes on each side, or until lightly browned. Brush with oil if the vegetables become dry.

Remove the vegetables from the oven and place them on a serving platter. Drizzle with the remaining 2 tablespoons oil, sprinkling with the remaining basil and parsley.

Makes 4 servings

Sprouted Lentil Salad

Salad

2   cups sprouted lentils
1   cup chopped tomatoes
¼   cup pitted black or green olives
¼   cup sliced celery
¼   cup chopped scallions

¼ cup finely chopped sweet red or yellow peppers
¼ cup chopped fresh parsley
½ cup alfalfa

Dressing

2 tablespoons olive oil
¼ teaspoon ground cumin
½ medium tomato
¼ medium cucumber, peeled
½ cup sunflower seeds, soaked and drained
Pinch of sea salt
Pinch of ground black pepper

TO MAKE THE SALAD: In a large bowl, toss together the lentils, tomatoes, olives, celery, scallions, peppers, parsley, and alfalfa.

TO MAKE THE DRESSING: In a blender or food processor, combine the oil, cumin, tomato, cucumber, sunflower seeds, salt, and pepper. Blend until creamy.

Pour the dressing over the salad ingredients and toss well. Refrigerate until ready to serve.

Makes 4 servings

Variation: Chickpea or mung bean sprouts can be used in place of the lentils.

Chickpea and Apple Salad

This salad is great served with warm pita bread.

Salad

3 cups cooked chickpeas
3 stalks celery, chopped
2 large apples, chopped (see note)
½ cup raisins, soaked in hot water and drained

Dressing

     2   tablespoons soy flour
     ¾   cup dry cider
     ¼   cup olive oil
     ¼   cup cider vinegar
         Chopped fresh cilantro

To make the salad: In a medium bowl, combine the chickpeas, celery, apples, and raisins. Toss together well and set aside.

To make the dressing: In a medium saucepan, stir together the flour and cider. Bring to a boil over medium-low heat. Simmer for 15 minutes, stirring often. Remove from the heat and let cool. Whisk in the oil and vinegar.

Pour the cider mixture over the chickpea salad and mix well. Sprinkle with the cilantro.

Makes 4 servings

Note: To prevent apples from turning brown, squeeze lemon juice over them immediately after cutting.

Roasted Red Pepper and Watercress Sandwiches

     3   sweet red peppers
     ¼   cup Tofu Mayonnaise (see page 69)
     4   slices whole-grain bread, lightly toasted
     1   cup watercress
     1   carrot, grated
     ½   cucumber, thinly sliced
         Pinch of sea salt
         Pinch of ground black pepper

Preheat the broiler.

In a large broiling pan, place the red peppers in the broiler about 4" from the heat, turning often so that all sides are evenly charred. Remove the peppers to a covered container for 5 minutes; the moisture released by the heat will make the skins easier to remove. Using a paring knife, peel the skin off and remove the seeds and ribs.

Spread the mayonnaise on 2 of the bread slices. Add the roasted peppers, watercress, carrots, and cucumbers in layers. Sprinkle with the salt and black pepper. Top with the remaining 2 slices of bread.

Makes 2

DINNER

STARTERS

Braised Fennel

2	large bulbs fennel
1	tablespoon extra-virgin olive oil
2	cloves garlic, chopped
2	tablespoons sesame seeds
¼	cup + 2 tablespoons vegetable stock
	Juice of 1 lemon
	Rind of 1 lemon, grated
	Pinch of sea salt
	Pinch of ground black pepper

Trim the fennel ends and feathery fronds, which can be used as a garnish. Remove any tough outer ribs. Halve and thinly slice the fennel lengthwise.

(continued)

In a medium skillet, warm the oil over medium heat. Add the fennel, garlic, and sesame seeds. Sauté until slightly brown, stirring constantly.

Add the stock, lemon juice, and half the lemon rind. Bring to a boil over medium heat, stirring often. Reduce the heat and simmer gently for 15 minutes.

Season with the salt, pepper, and the remaining lemon rind. Serve warm.

Makes 4 servings

Chicory and Bean Salad

Salad

2	cups chopped chicory
1½	cups cooked white beans (preferably navy beans)
2	green peppers, finely diced
4	scallions, chopped
8	black olives, pitted and chopped
2	large tomatoes, seeded and diced
¼	cup chopped fresh parsley
2	tablespoons minced chives
1	teaspoon chopped fresh thyme

Dressing

2–3	cloves garlic, minced
2	tablespoons mustard
¼	cup wine vinegar
¼	cup + 2 tablespoons olive oil

TO MAKE THE SALAD: Place the chicory on a large serving plate.

In a large bowl, combine the beans, peppers, scallions, olives, tomatoes, parsley, chives, and thyme. Toss well. Spoon the bean mixture onto the bed of chicory.

To make the dressing: In a small bowl, combine the garlic, mustard, vinegar, and oil. Whisk well and pour over the bean mixture.

Makes 4 servings

Chilled Spicy Cucumber Soup

4   large cucumbers, peeled, seeded, and cubed
3   scallions, chopped
2   teaspoons chopped garlic
1   teaspoon chopped fresh ginger
1   teaspoon ground cumin
1   teaspoon ground coriander
    Pinch of ground cinnamon
    Pinch of sea salt
    Pinch of ground black pepper
2   tablespoons chopped fresh mint
1   tablespoon rice syrup
3   cups plain or soy yogurt
3   cups fresh carrot juice or vegetable stock, chilled
2   teaspoons olive oil
2   tablespoons mustard seeds
    Chopped fresh chives

In a large bowl, combine the cucumbers, scallions, garlic, ginger, cumin, coriander, cinnamon, salt, pepper, mint, and syrup. Toss together and chill in the refrigerator for 30 minutes to 2 hours. Transfer the mixture to a blender or food processor. Blend until pureed.

Pour the puree into a large bowl. Add the yogurt and juice or stock. Whisk together well.

In a medium skillet, warm the oil over medium heat. Add the mustard seeds. Cook, stirring constantly, until the seeds pop. Pour over the soup.

Serve chilled with the chives sprinkled on top.

Makes 4 to 6 servings

Italian Bread Salad

Salad

4   cups cubed whole-wheat bread
1   small red onion, sliced
1   head lettuce, torn into bite-size pieces
1   cup chopped, peeled cucumbers
1   cup diced carrots
½   cup chopped radishes
1   cup sliced mushrooms
4   scallions, sliced
¼   cup black or green olives, pitted
2   tablespoons capers
2   cloves garlic, minced
2   tablespoons chopped fresh parsley

Dressing

¼   cup + 1 tablespoon extra-virgin olive oil
2   tablespoons orange juice
3   tablespoons balsamic vinegar
   Pinch of sea salt
   Pinch of ground black pepper

To make the salad: In a medium bowl, soak the bread cubes in water for 30 minutes. In a small bowl, soak the onions in water for 40 minutes.

In a large bowl, combine the lettuce, cucumbers, carrots, radishes, mushrooms, scallions, olives, capers, garlic, and parsley. Toss well.

Drain the onions. Pat dry and add to the salad bowl. Squeeze the water from the bread cubes and crumble them over the salad.

To make the dressing: In a small bowl, combine the oil, orange juice, vinegar, salt, and pepper. Whisk together.

Pour the dressing over the salad and toss. Serve chilled.

Makes 4 servings

Cool Avocado Soup

3 tablespoons extra-virgin olive oil
½ cup diced onions
2 cloves garlic, chopped
6 scallions, chopped
  Pinch of ground cumin
  Pinch of sea salt
2 potatoes, cut into small cubes
4 cups vegetable stock
2 avocado, peeled and cubed
¼ cup lime juice
  About ¾ cup soy or plain yogurt
2 tablespoons chopped fresh cilantro
2 tablespoons minced sweet red pepper

In a medium skillet, warm the oil over medium heat. Add the onions, garlic, scallions, cumin, and salt. Sauté until soft but not brown.

Add the potatoes to the skillet and stir together. Add the stock. Cover and simmer for 15 to 20 minutes, or until the potatoes are soft. Remove from the heat and let cool.

In a blender or food processor, combine the avocado and lime juice. Blend well. Add the potatoes, yogurt, and cilantro. Puree until creamy. If the soup seems too thick, add more yogurt to thin the consistency.

Transfer the mixture into a large bowl. Cover and chill in the refrigerator for at least 2 hours before serving. Garnish with the red peppers.

Makes 4 to 6 servings

ENTRÉES

Gado Gado

This dish is an Indonesian favorite consisting of raw and slightly cooked vegetables.

Vegetables

4	medium potatoes
3	carrots, sliced diagonally into thin pieces
1	cup cauliflower florets
12	snow or sugar snap peas, halved
	Tamari
¼	cup cubed firm tofu, drained
6	radishes, sliced
½	small cabbage, shredded
2	cups mung bean sprouts
6	scallions, chopped
	Chopped fresh cilantro

Sauce

2	tablespoons vegetable oil
1	onion, finely chopped
3	cloves garlic, chopped
2	teaspoons chopped fresh ginger
2	stalks celery, chopped
1	tablespoon sugar
	Juice of 1 lemon
¾	cup crunchy peanut butter or other nut butter
¼	cup coconut milk
	Tamari
¼	teaspoon ground red pepper
1	cup vegetable stock

To MAKE THE VEGETABLES: In a large pot, combine the potatoes and enough water to cover. Bring to a boil over medium-high heat. On a steaming rack set over the boiling potatoes, steam the carrots, cauliflower, and peas for about 5 minutes, or until crisp-tender. Drain the potatoes and run them under cold water. Slice thinly.

In a small skillet, sprinkle some tamari over the tofu cubes. Cook, stirring often, until slightly brown on all sides. Remove from the heat and let cool.

When the cooked vegetables are cool enough to handle, arrange them with the raw vegetables on individual plates. Start by placing the radishes and cabbage in the middle of the plates and arrange the potatoes in a circle around them. Alternate with the carrots and cauliflower. Arrange the tofu cubes and peas over the cabbage. Sprinkle with the sprouts, scallions, and cilantro.

To MAKE THE SAUCE: In a medium skillet, warm the oil over medium heat. Add the onions, garlic, and ginger. Sauté until the onions are translucent. Add the celery and stir well. Cook until slightly brown. Reduce the heat to low.

Add the sugar, lemon juice, peanut or other nut butter, coconut milk, tamari, red pepper, and stock. Cook, stirring constantly, until the peanut or nut butter melts completely. If the sauce is too thick, add water or more stock.

Serve the salad with the warm sauce on the side.

Makes 4 to 6 servings

Savory Stuffed Tomatoes and Pureed Pumpkin

Stuffed Tomatoes

4	large tomatoes
1	tablespoon sunflower oil
1	cup chopped onions
1	clove garlic, crushed
	Pinch of sea salt
	Pinch of ground black pepper
½	teaspoon ground cumin
½	teaspoon ground coriander
1	green or sweet red pepper, diced
2	cups cooked kidney beans
2	tablespoons flour mixed with enough water to form a paste
1	teaspoon balsamic vinegar
1	bay leaf
¼	cup fresh chopped cilantro

Preheat the oven to 350°F. Coat a shallow baking dish with nonstick cooking spray.

Cut the tomatoes at the top and carefully scoop out the pulp and seeds. Reserve for later use. Cut a very thin slice from the bottom of each tomato so that the tomatoes can stand upright without toppling over.

In a large saucepan, warm the oil over medium heat. Add the onions, garlic, salt, and black pepper. Sauté for 2 to 3 minutes. Add the cumin, coriander, and green or sweet red peppers. Cook for 4 to 5 minutes, stirring often. Add the beans, flour paste, vinegar, and bay leaf. Mix well. Reduce the heat to low. Cook for 5 to 6 minutes, stirring often. If the mixture gets too dry, add a little of the reserved tomato pulp. Stir in the cilantro. Remove from the heat and let cool. Remove the bay leaf.

Fill the tomatoes with the bean mixture and place in the baking dish. Bake for 15 to 20 minutes. Serve warm as a side dish.

Makes 4 to 6 servings

Corn and Pumpkin Meal

1½	cups peeled, cubed pumpkin
2¼	cups water
1	cup cornmeal
½	teaspoon maple syrup
	Pinch of sea salt
	Pinch of ground black pepper
2	tablespoons roasted peanuts
¼	cup chopped scallions

In a medium pot of boiling water, cook the pumpkin until tender. Drain, reserving the cooking water. Mash the pumpkin with a fork or electric mixer.

In a large pot, bring the 2¼ cups water to a boil over medium-high heat. Pour in the cornmeal. Cook, stirring frequently, until it forms an oatmeal-like porridge. Add the pumpkin, syrup, salt, and pepper. Stir together well. Add the reserved cooking water to thin, as needed.

Just before serving, sprinkle with the peanuts and scallions.

Makes about 4 cups

Vegetable Mousse and Pungent Corn Pasta

Cilantro and Broad Bean Mousse with Paprika Sauce

This mousse is good served over a few slices of fresh tomato.

Mousse

1	tablespoon black sesame seeds
2	tablespoons olive oil
½	cup diced onions
2	cloves garlic, crushed
1	teaspoon ground cumin
	Pinch of sea salt
	Pinch of ground black pepper
3	cups broad beans, cooked and skinned
2	tablespoons chopped fresh cilantro
1	teaspoon lemon juice
1	tablespoon agar–agar, dissolved in ¼ cup water

Sauce

2	tablespoons olive oil
1	teaspoon cumin seeds
1	shallot, finely chopped
1	clove garlic, crushed
1	sweet red pepper, chopped
1	tomato, seeded and chopped
	Pinch of sea salt
¼	cup white wine or nonalcoholic white wine
½	teaspoon paprika
1	teaspoon tomato puree
½	cup vegetable stock
1	tablespoon chopped fresh parsley

To make the mousse: Lightly coat 4 individual baking dishes with nonstick spray and line the bottoms with grease-proof paper sheets. Sprinkle ¼ tablespoon of the sesame seeds on the bottom of each dish.

In a medium skillet, warm the oil over medium heat. Add the onions. Sauté for 5 minutes. Add the garlic, cumin, salt, and pepper. Reduce the heat to low and cook for 2 to 3 minutes. Remove from the heat and let cool.

In a blender or food processor, combine the onions, beans, cilantro, and lemon juice. Blend until well-pureed. Transfer the mixture into a large bowl.

In a small skillet, warm the dissolved agar-agar over low heat, taking care not to bring it to a boil. Pour into the bowl with the bean mixture. Stir until well-mixed. Spoon into the baking dishes. Cover and refrigerate overnight.

To make the sauce: In a medium saucepan, warm the oil over medium heat. Add the cumin seeds and sauté for 2 minutes. Add the shallots, garlic, and red peppers. Cook until softened. Add the tomatoes, salt, wine or nonalcoholic wine, and paprika. Cook over medium-high heat for 3 to 4 minutes to reduce the wine. Add the tomato puree and vegetable stock. Bring to a boil. Reduce the heat and simmer for 5 to 10 minutes. Remove from the heat and let cool.

In a blender or food processor, combine the sauce and the parsley. Blend until smooth.

Turn out the mousse onto individual plates, removing the grease-proof paper. Spoon the sauce over the mousse.

Makes 4 servings

Note: To give the sauce a creamy texture, you can add ¼ cup soy cream while it is still warm. You can also pass the sauce through a sieve to get out any lumps.

Corn Pasta

Pasta

2	cups corn pasta (see note)
½	cup finely chopped scallions
¼	cup chopped sun-dried tomatoes
½	cup chopped carrots
1	cup watercress

Dressing

¼	cup extra-virgin olive oil
2	cloves garlic, crushed
¼	cup pine nuts, toasted
¼	cup chopped fresh parsley
1	teaspoon lemon juice
1	tablespoon tomato puree
2	tablespoons water

TO MAKE THE PASTA: In a large pot of boiling water, cook the pasta according to the package directions. Drain.

In a large bowl, combine the pasta, scallions, tomatoes, carrots, and watercress. Toss together until well-mixed.

TO MAKE THE DRESSING: In a medium bowl, combine the oil, garlic, nuts, parsley, lemon juice, tomato puree, and water. Whisk together. Pour the dressing over the pasta. Toss thoroughly. Serve warm or at room temperature.

Makes 4 servings

Note: Corn pasta is available at health food stores and in the Spanish foods section of some supermarkets.

Puree of Beets
with Vegetable-Rice Salad

Beet Mousse

3–4	beets, peeled and diced
4	cups soy milk
¼	cup chopped walnuts
2	tablespoons soy sauce
2½	tablespoons agar-agar, dissolved in ½ cup water
	Lemon slices (optional)

In a large saucepan, combine the beets and soy milk. Bring to a boil over medium heat. Reduce the heat to medium-low and simmer for 45 to 60 minutes, or until tender.

In a blender or food processor, combine the beet mixture, nuts, and soy sauce. Blend until smooth. Transfer the mixture into a large bowl.

In a small saucepan, warm the dissolved agar-agar over low heat for 3 to 4 minutes, or until warm but not boiling. Transfer into the bowl with the beets. Whisk together thoroughly.

Pour into individual serving dishes. Chill for a couple hours or overnight to set. Serve with lemon slices, if desired.

Makes 4 servings

Rice Salad

Salad

2	cups cooked, cooled rice
4	scallions, chopped
½	cup cooked mung beans
½	cup finely chopped carrots, steamed
½	cup fresh peas, steamed

(continued)

½   cup halved cherry tomatoes
3   tablespoons sunflower oil
     Pinch of sea salt
     Pinch of ground black pepper

Dressing

½   cup fresh corn kernels, roasted
½   cup roasted cashews
1   teaspoon grated fresh ginger
¼   cup + 2 tablespoons light oil
1   clove garlic, chopped
2   tablespoons tamari
1   tablespoon cilantro
     Juice of ½ lemon
     About ¼ cup water

TO MAKE THE SALAD: In a large bowl, combine the rice, scallions, beans, carrots, peas, tomatoes, oil, salt, and pepper. Mix well. Chill for at least 1 hour.

TO MAKE THE DRESSING: In a blender or food processor, combine the corn, cashews, ginger, oil, garlic, tamari, cilantro, lemon juice, and water. Blend until smooth. Add more water if too thick. Pour the dressing over the rice mixture. Serve at room temperature.

Makes 4 servings

Broccoli-Cauliflower Bake with Butter Beans

Baked Broccoli and Cauliflower with Tofu Sauce

½   cup small cauliflower florets
2   cups broccoli florets
½   cup crumbled firm tofu, drained

2   tablespoons sunflower oil
2   tablespoons soy sauce
1   teaspoon dry mustard
¼   cup sunflower seeds

Preheat the oven to 350°F.

In a large pot of boiling water, add the cauliflower. Cook for 5 to 8 minutes, or until tender, not mushy. Remove from the boiling water and immediately place in a pan of cold water to keep crisp. Reserve the cooking water.

Add the broccoli to the pot of boiling water. Cook for 3 to 4 minutes. Remove from the boiling water and plunge into cold water. Reserve the cooking water.

In a blender or food processor, combine the tofu, 6 tablespoons of the reserved cooking water, the oil, soy sauce, and mustard. Blend until creamy.

Arrange the cauliflower and broccoli in a baking dish. Pour the tofu sauce on top and sprinkle with the sunflower seeds. Bake for 20 minutes, or until lightly browned.

Makes 4 servings

Butter Beans in Onion Gravy

¼   cup olive oil
1   cup finely chopped red onions
2   cups halved mushrooms
¼   teaspoon dried rosemary
    Pinch of sea salt
    Pinch of ground black pepper
1   tablespoon whole-wheat flour
2   tablespoons white miso
¾   cup vegetable stock
2   cups cooked butter beans
    Chopped fresh parsley

In a medium skillet, warm the oil over medium heat. Add the onions. Sauté until slightly brown. Add the mushrooms, rosemary, salt, and pepper. Cook for 6 to 8 minutes.

Stir in the flour and cook, stirring often, until it turns brown. Remove the pan from the heat. Stir in the miso and stock. Mix well. Return the skillet to the heat. Bring to a boil over medium heat and simmer for 5 minutes.

Add the beans. Simmer for another 8 to 10 minutes. Sprinkle with the parsley.

Makes 4 servings

Chapter 7

LATE SUMMER

A LTHOUGH IT IS NOT STRICTLY RECOGNIZED as a season, late summer is the time when the yang energy slowly turns into the yin quality that will characterize the autumn and winter months. This is the point of transition between the radiance and expansion of summer and the cooler, more mysterious end of summer, which announces the autumn to come. There is a timeless, dreamlike, magical quality about this time of year. We return from our vacations and prepare for the cooler seasons ahead. It is the time for solitary or intimate walks in forests, wearing an extra layer of clothing after sunset. In certain parts of Europe and the United States, late summer is a time of storms, dangerous sea tides, and rains. This is the time for contemplation, so allow change to come slowly into your life, relationships, and activities.

To attune to late summer, the diet should contain more cooked foods, more protein, fewer dairy foods, and the right combination of carbohydrates.

Late summer cooking methods: Boiling, grilling, sautéing, and simmering.

Late summer vegetables: Squash, tomatoes, zucchini, carrots, cabbage, peas, chestnuts, corn, sweet potatoes, pumpkin, and parsnips.

Late summer grains: Most varieties of legumes.

Late summer fruits: Apples, grapes, chestnuts, and apricots.

Special late summer foods: Onions, leeks, ginger, cinnamon, fennel, cooked fruits, barley malt, molasses, and rice syrup.

Suggested late summer body therapies: Loosening and stretching exercises, centering meditations, breathing exercises, and contemplative walking.

Suggested late summer diet: Rice salads, pastas, grain croquettes, buckwheat pancakes, scrambled tofu, and tempeh sandwiches.

LUNCH

Green Bean Salad

12	pearl onions, peeled
3	tablespoons extra-virgin olive oil
1	tablespoon confectioners' sugar
¼	cup balsamic vinegar
¼	cup + 2 tablespoons vegetable stock
2	cups sliced French green beans, with ends removed
2	cups sliced jicama
¼	cup chopped sun-dried tomatoes
	Pinch of sea salt
	Pinch of ground black pepper
	Lettuce

In a small saucepan over medium-high heat, boil enough water to cover the onions. Add the onions and boil for 1 minute. Remove from the heat and drain.

In a medium skillet, warm the oil over medium heat. Add the onions. Sauté until lightly browned. Add the sugar and vinegar. Cook, stirring often, until the onions caramelize. Pour in the stock. Reduce the heat to low and simmer for 5 minutes.

Meanwhile, in a large pot of boiling water, blanch the beans for about 4 minutes. Drain and run them under cold water. Add the beans, jicama, tomatoes, salt, and pepper to the onion mixture. Mix well.

Remove from the heat. Serve immediately over the lettuce.

Makes 4 to 6 servings

Lunchtime Rice Noodle Salad

Marinade

¼	cup cider vinegar
¼	cup tamari
1	clove garlic, chopped
1	teaspoon grated fresh ginger

Salad

1½	cups cubed firm tofu, drained
4	tablespoons sesame oil
2	packages (6 ounces each) rice noodles
2	tablespoons tamari
2	tablespoons lemon juice
6	scallions, chopped
1	cup sliced zucchini
½	cup bean sprouts
½	cup thinly sliced seeded cucumbers
½	cup chopped fresh herbs

TO MAKE THE MARINADE: In a small bowl, combine the vinegar, tamari, garlic, and ginger. Whisk together until well-blended.

TO MAKE THE SALAD: Add the tofu to the marinade and refrigerate for at least 2 hours, or overnight (a glass container works best as it does

(continued)

not retain or add flavors or odors). Drain the tofu, reserving the marinade.

In a medium skillet, warm 2 tablespoons of the oil over medium heat. Add the tofu and the marinade. Sauté until the tofu turns slightly brown. Cook for 2 more minutes. Remove from the heat and let cool. Transfer the tofu into a large bowl.

In a large pot of boiling water, cook the noodles according to the package directions until they are al dente. Drain. Transfer into the bowl with the tofu. Add the remaining 2 tablespoons of oil, the tamari, and lemon juice. Toss well. Mix in the scallions, zucchini, sprouts, and cucumbers. Add the herbs. Toss together until thoroughly mixed. Serve at room temperature.

Makes 4 to 6 servings

Tabbouleh

2	cups couscous
4	cups boiling water
¾	cup raisins, soaked in hot water and drained
½	medium cucumber, peeled, seeded, and coarsely chopped
6	scallions, sliced
8	cherry tomatoes, halved
1	cup green peas, steamed
¼	cup chopped dried apricots
3	tablespoons chopped fresh mint
½	cup chopped fresh parsley
1	teaspoon sea salt
1	teaspoon ground cumin
¼	cup + 2 tablespoons lemon juice
¼	cup olive oil

In a large heatproof bowl, combine the couscous and boiling water. Stir together. Let it stand, covered, for 30 minutes, or until all the water is absorbed. Stir occasionally.

Uncover the couscous and fluff with a fork. Add the raisins, cucumbers, scallions, tomatoes, peas, and apricots. Toss together. Stir in the mint, parsley, salt, cumin, lemon juice, and oil until well-mixed. Serve chilled.

Makes 4 to 6 servings

Wheat Berry Salad

Salad

1	cup wheat berries (see note)
1	cup mung beans
2	stalks celery, finely chopped
2	carrots, finely chopped
½	cup chopped fresh parsley
	Pinch of sea salt
	Pinch of ground black pepper

Dressing

¼	cup olive oil
¼	cup lemon juice
3	cloves garlic, chopped
¼	cup chopped scallions
2	tablespoons soy sauce
½	teaspoon mustard
1	teaspoon ground cinnamon

To make the salad: In a medium saucepan, combine the wheat berries with enough water to cover. Bring to a boil over medium–high heat. Reduce the heat to medium and simmer, covered, for about 1 hour, or until all the water is absorbed and the grains are tender. Check occasionally, adding water to cover, if needed.

In a medium pot of boiling water, cook the beans for about 20 minutes. Remove from the heat and drain.

(continued)

In a large bowl, combine the wheat berries, beans, celery, carrots, parsley, salt, and pepper. Toss together well.

TO MAKE THE DRESSING: In a medium bowl, combine the oil, lemon juice, garlic, scallions, soy sauce, mustard, and cinnamon. Whisk well.

Pour the dressing over the salad. Toss and let stand for 1 hour or overnight in the refrigerator for the flavors to blend.

Makes 4 to 6 servings

Note: Wheat berries are whole, unprocessed kernels, available at health food stores.

Wild Rice and Quinoa Salad

This dish is good served with a tomato and cucumber salad.

½	cup wild rice, rinsed
4	cups water
1	teaspoon + 1 tablespoon sea salt
½	cup quinoa
1	small sweet red pepper
2	tablespoons sunflower oil
2	cups sliced wild mushrooms
2	cloves garlic, crushed
2	tablespoons chopped fresh parsley
	Pinch of ground black pepper
¼	cup toasted pumpkin seeds

Preheat the broiler.

In a medium saucepan, combine the rice and 3 cups of the water. Bring to a boil over medium-high heat. Reduce the heat to medium and simmer for 45 minutes to 1 hour, or until tender. Add more water, if needed. Remove from the heat and let stand.

In another medium saucepan, bring the remaining 1 cup water and 1 teaspoon of the salt to a boil. Add the quinoa. Cover, reduce the heat to low, and cook for 15 minutes. Remove from the heat and let stand.

In a large broiling pan, place the red pepper in the broiler about 4" from the heat, turning often so that all sides are evenly charred. Remove the pepper to a covered container for 5 minutes; the moisture released by the heat will make the skin easier to remove. Using a paring knife, peel the skin off, remove the seeds and ribs, and chop the pepper.

In a medium skillet, warm the oil over medium heat. Add the remaining 1 tablespoon salt, the mushrooms, garlic, parsley, and black pepper. Sauté for 4 to 5 minutes, stirring continuously. Remove from the heat.

In a large bowl, combine the roasted peppers, mushrooms, and pumpkin seeds. Mix well. Add the rice and quinoa. Toss together well. Serve immediately or at room temperature.

Makes 4 to 6 servings

DINNER

STARTERS

Baked Spring Rolls

Filling

2   tablespoons sesame oil
1   teaspoon grated fresh ginger
1   leek, finely sliced
1   white onion, finely sliced
2   cups shredded carrots

(continued)

2	cups shredded green cabbage
2	cups bean sprouts
4	scallions, chopped
¼	cup tamari
1	teaspoon ground black pepper
1	teaspoon rice wine vinegar
1	package rice paper wrappers (see note)
	Olive oil

Sauce

1	tablespoon tamari
2	tablespoons cider vinegar
2	cloves garlic, chopped
3	tablespoons chopped roasted peanuts
½	tablespoon Dijon mustard
2	teaspoons honey
1	tablespoon water
1	tablespoon chopped scallions
	Lettuce (optional)
	Mint leaves (optional)

Preheat oven to 350°F. Coat a large baking sheet with nonstick cooking spray.

TO MAKE THE FILLING: In a large wok, warm the oil over medium heat. Add the ginger, leeks, and onions. Stir-fry for several minutes. Add the carrots and cabbage. Stir-fry briefly. Add the sprouts and scallions. Cook, stirring, for 5 minutes. Add the tamari, pepper, and vinegar. Mix well. Transfer the vegetables to a large bowl and set aside to cool.

Fill a medium bowl with warm water. Dip one of the rice wrappers briefly into the water to soften. Remove from the water and drain on a dish towel. Put about 2 tablespoons of the filling in a lump in the center of the wrapper. Fold in each side and roll tightly—the wrapper will seal on its own. Repeat until all the filling is used. Keep the rolls under a moist dish towel until ready to bake.

Lightly brush the rolls with a little oil. Bake for about 3 minutes on each side, turning gently with tongs or two forks.

To make the sauce: In a small bowl, combine the tamari, vinegar, garlic, peanuts, mustard, honey, water, and scallions. Whisk together until well-blended.

Serve the rolls sliced with the dipping sauce. Garnish with lettuce and mint leaves (if using).

Makes 4 to 6 servings

Note: Rice paper wrappers are sold frozen in Asian supermarkets.

Soy Falafel

Serve this dish with Hummus (see page 71) and a salad.

2	tablespoons sesame oil
1	cup chopped onions
3	cups crumbled firm tofu, drained
1	cup dried bread crumbs
¼	cup chopped fresh parsley
2	tablespoons tamari
4	cloves garlic, chopped
1	tablespoon ground cumin
1	tablespoon ground coriander
¼	cup tahini
¼	cup lemon juice
	Pinch of sea salt
	Pinch of ground black pepper

Preheat the oven to 350°F. Lightly coat a baking sheet with nonstick cooking spray.

In a small skillet, warm the oil over medium heat. Add the onions. Sauté, stirring often, until tender. Remove from the heat.

In a large bowl, toss together the onions, tofu, and bread crumbs. Add the parsley, tamari, garlic, cumin, coriander, tahini, lemon juice, salt, and

(continued)

pepper. Mix well. With your hands, roll the mixture into 2" balls and place on the prepared baking sheet.

Bake for 20 minutes, or until evenly browned on all sides, turning them often. Serve warm.

Makes 4 to 6 servings

Yam and Walnut Salad

3	cups diced yams or sweet potatoes
½	teaspoon sea salt
½	teaspoon sugar
¼	cup dried juniper berries, soaked in hot water and drained (see note)
¼	cup chopped roasted walnuts
¼	cup golden raisins, soaked in hot water and drained
¼	cup maple syrup
¼	cup water
1	teaspoon ground red pepper
2	tablespoons fruit juice
2	tablespoons lemon juice
	Chopped fresh cilantro

In a large pot of boiling water, blanch the yams or sweet potatoes with the salt and sugar for 8 to 10 minutes. Drain and run them under cold water. Transfer the yams to a large bowl. Add the berries, nuts, and raisins. Toss together.

In a medium saucepan, warm the syrup, water, and pepper over medium heat for 5 to 7 minutes, or until the liquid is reduced by half. Remove from the heat and cool briefly.

Add the syrup mixture, fruit juice, lemon juice, and cilantro to the bowl. Toss well until the juices cover the salad evenly. Serve chilled or at room temperature.

Makes 4 to 6 servings

Note: Dried juniper berries are available at health food stores.

Potato Cakes with Spinach Sauce

Potato Cakes

1	tablespoon sunflower oil
1	cup diced red onions or leeks
2	cups cubed boiled potatoes
30	black or green olives, pitted and chopped
¼	cup chopped sun-dried tomatoes
¼	cup capers, drained
1	cup soft bread crumbs
¼	cup fresh parsley
	Pinch of sea salt
	Pinch of ground black pepper
2	egg whites, beaten

Sauce

4	cups chopped spinach
¼	cup soy milk
½	teaspoon ground nutmeg
	Pinch of sea salt
	Pinch of ground black pepper

To make the potato cakes: In a medium skillet, warm the oil over medium heat. Add the onions or leeks. Sauté until tender. Remove from the heat and set aside to cool.

In a large bowl, mash the potatoes with a fork, leaving a few small lumps. Add the onions or leeks, olives, tomatoes, capers, and ½ cup of the bread crumbs. Season with the parsley, salt, and pepper. Mix well.

Using your hands, shape the potato mixture into ½"-thick patties, the size of small hamburgers. In a small bowl, dip the patties into the egg whites. Sprinkle with the remaining ½ cup bread crumbs.

In a medium skillet, cook the patties over medium heat for 5 minutes on each side, or until evenly browned.

(continued)

To make the sauce: On a steaming rack over a large pot of boiling water, steam the spinach for 2 to 3 minutes.

In a blender or food processor, combine the spinach, soy milk, nutmeg, salt, and pepper. Blend well.

Warm the sauce in a small saucepan over medium heat. Remove from the heat and spoon onto serving plates. Place the potato cakes on top.

Makes 4 to 6 servings

Eggplant Crostini

1	small baguette or medium loaf of Italian bread
1	clove garlic
4	tablespoons + 2 teaspoons olive oil
1	small eggplant, thinly sliced
1	cup sun-dried tomatoes
2	tablespoons chopped fresh basil
1	teaspoon sea salt
1	teaspoon ground black pepper

Slice the baguette or Italian bread into thin slices. Rub each slice with the garlic and brush lightly with 1 tablespoon of the oil. Toast on both sides.

Coat the eggplant slices well with 3 tablespoons of the oil. In a medium skillet, grill the eggplant on both sides until brown. Remove from the heat. Lay the eggplant slices on the bread slices.

In a blender or food processor, puree the tomatoes and 1 teaspoon of the oil. If the mixture is too thick, add water by the tablespoon to thin. The puree should be the consistency of hummus. Top each of the eggplant slices evenly with a spoonful of the puree. Sprinkle evenly with the basil, salt, and pepper.

Return to the skillet and grill for 2 minutes. Serve warm with the remaining oil.

Makes 4 to 6 servings

ENTRÉES

Rice-Stuffed Squash with Tomato Sauce

Squash

1	large green or yellow summer squash
	Sea salt

Filling

4	tablespoons sunflower oil
1	cup chopped onions
1	clove garlic, chopped
1	stalk celery, chopped
1	cup sliced mushrooms
2	teaspoons mild curry powder
	Pinch of sea salt
2	small carrots, diced and steamed
¼	cup green peas, steamed
1½	cups cooked brown rice
¼	cup chopped fresh parsley
2	tablespoons chopped hazelnuts
	Pinch of ground black pepper

Sauce

¼	cup sunflower oil
1	cup chopped red onions
	Pinch of sea salt
	Pinch of ground black pepper
1	clove garlic, chopped
½	teaspoon dried oregano
6	medium tomatoes, peeled, seeded, and chopped
¼	cup black olives, pitted
2	tablespoons capers
½	red chili pepper, seeded, and chopped (optional), see note

Preheat the oven to 350°F.

TO PREPARE THE SQUASH: Cut the squash in half lengthwise and scoop out the seeds. Sprinkle with a little salt and leave upside down to drain for 15 to 20 minutes. On a steaming rack over a large pot of boiling water, steam the squash for 15 minutes. Wipe dry and set aside.

TO MAKE THE FILLING: In a wok, warm 2 tablespoons of the oil over medium heat. Add the onions and garlic. Sauté until tender. Stir in the celery, mushrooms, curry, and salt. Stir-fry until vegetables become soft. Add the carrots and peas. Mix well. Stir in the rice, parsley, nuts, and pepper. Remove from the heat.

Press the filling into one half of the squash. Top with the other half. To keep together, use toothpicks that have been soaked in water.

Brush the squash with the remaining 2 tablespoons oil and place on a baking sheet. Bake for 30 to 40 minutes.

TO MAKE THE SAUCE: In a medium skillet, warm the oil over medium heat. Add the onions, salt, black pepper, garlic, and oregano. Sauté for 3 to 4 minutes, stirring often. Add the tomatoes and cook for 3 minutes more. Add the olives, capers, and chili peppers (if using). Simmer for 15 to 20 minutes, or until the sauce is thick.

Serve the sauce over the squash.

Makes 4 to 6 servings

Note: Wear plastic gloves when handling the chili pepper.
Variation: Instead of thickening the sauce for the last 15 to 20 minutes in the saucepan, the sauce can be poured over the squash and baked.

Panzerotti and Glazed Beets

Vegetable Panzerotti

1	tablespoon + ½ cup olive oil
2	cups spinach
2	cloves garlic, crushed
1	tablespoon capers
¼	cup pitted, chopped black olives
2	tablespoons crushed roasted walnuts
1	tablespoon chopped raisins, soaked in hot water and drained
	Whole-Wheat Pizza Dough (see page 91)
1	egg, beaten

In a medium skillet, warm 1 tablespoon of the oil over medium heat. Add the spinach and cook for 5 to 6 minutes. Remove from the heat.

Chop the cooked spinach and place in a medium bowl. Add the garlic, capers, olives, nuts, and raisins. Mix well.

Lightly flour a clean work surface. With a rolling pin, roll out the pizza dough until very thin. Cut the dough into circles using a cookie cutter. Place 1 tablespoon of the spinach filling in the middle of each circle, leaving the edges clean. Brush the egg along the edge of each circle. Fold in half and seal the edges well by pressing down with a fork.

In a medium skillet, warm the remaining ½ cup oil over medium heat. Cook the panzerotti until golden brown on both sides.

Makes 4 to 6 servings

Variation: For a healthier approach, instead of sautéing the panzerotti, you can bake it in a preheated oven at 350°F for 15 to 20 minutes.

Glazed Beets

3	cups peeled, grated beets
¼	cup dry red wine or nonalcoholic red wine
2	tablespoons cider vinegar

(continued)

1 tablespoon sugar
2 tablespoons sunflower oil
2 tablespoons golden raisins or cranberries, soaked in
water
Pinch of sea salt
Pinch of ground black pepper
Orange rind

Preheat the oven to 350°F.

In a medium bowl, stir together the beets, wine, vinegar, sugar, oil, raisins or cranberries, salt, and pepper. Transfer into a baking dish and cover with a lid or foil.

Bake for 20 to 30 minutes, stirring occasionally. Garnish with the orange rind before serving.

Makes 4 to 6 servings

Japanese-Style Tofu with Assorted Vegetables

Teriyaki Tofu

2 blocks firm or smoked tofu, drained and cubed
¾ cup tamari
½ cup white wine or nonalcoholic white wine
½ cup grated onions
¼ cup honey
6 cloves garlic, chopped
1 tablespoon grated fresh ginger
1 teaspoon dry mustard
Pinch of ground black pepper

Preheat the broiler.

Place the tofu in the broiler about 4" from the heat. Broil until browned on all sides. Remove from the oven and set aside on a warm serving plate.

In a medium saucepan, combine the tamari, wine, onions, honey, garlic, ginger, mustard, and pepper. Bring to a boil over medium–high heat, stirring often. Reduce the heat to medium and simmer for 5 to 8 minutes.

Pour the marinade over the tofu cubes. Toss well and let the tofu sit, covered, overnight in the refrigerator. Serve chilled or at room temperature.

Makes 4 to 6 servings

Grilled Dressed Vegetables

Vegetables

10	mushrooms, halved
1	sweet red pepper, cut into wedges
10	button onions, peeled and parboiled
1	cup cubed winter squash, boiled for 5 minutes
8	cherry tomatoes
	Olive oil

Dressing

1	scallion, chopped
2	tablespoons sunflower oil
1	tablespoon chopped fresh parsley
1	tablespoon chopped fresh thyme
1	tablespoon Dijon mustard
1	tablespoon sherry vinegar

To make the vegetables: Brush the mushrooms, peppers, onions, squash, and tomatoes lightly with olive oil. In a large skillet over medium heat, cook the vegetables until lightly brown. Remove from the heat and transfer into a large bowl.

To make the dressing: In a blender or food processor, combine the scallions, oil, parsley, thyme, mustard, and vinegar. Process until well–blended. Pour the dressing over the vegetables. Toss together well.

Makes 4 to 6 servings

(continued)

Variation: Instead of cooking the vegetables in a skillet, you can place them on a broiling pan in a preheated oven and broil them about 4" from the heat until evenly browned.

Spanish Rice and Crisp Salad

Paella

2	tablespoons olive oil
1	cup chopped onions
2	cloves garlic, crushed
½	cup long-grain brown rice
½	cup chopped cashews
½	teaspoon ground paprika
½	teaspoon ground turmeric
1	teaspoon chopped fresh basil
1	sweet red pepper, chopped
1	green pepper, chopped
4	stalks celery, diced
2	medium zucchini, diced
1	large carrot, diced
½	cup green peas
5	tomatoes, skinned, seeded, and pureed
3	cups vegetable stock
1	tablespoon small green olives, pitted
	Lemon wedges
1	hard-boiled egg, sliced (optional)
	Chopped fresh parsley
	Sea salt
	Ground black pepper

In a large saucepan, warm the oil over medium heat. Add the onions and garlic. Sauté for 2 to 3 minutes, or until tender. Add the rice, cashews, paprika, and turmeric. Mix well and cook, stirring often, for 2 to 3 minutes more. Stir in the basil, red and green peppers, celery, zucchini, carrots, and peas.

Pour the tomatoes and stock into the pan. Mix well. Simmer for 35 to 40 minutes, or until the vegetables and rice are tender and the liquid has evaporated.

Serve warm and garnish with the olives, lemons, eggs, and parsley. Salt and pepper to taste.

Makes 4 to 6 servings

Summer Salad

1	small head lettuce, torn into bite-size pieces
3	stalks celery, chopped
¼	large cucumber, diced
1	medium avocado, coarsely chopped
2	medium tomatoes, sliced
1	bunch scallions, sliced
	Lemon Vinaigrette (see page 83)

In a large bowl, combine the lettuce, celery, cucumbers, avocado, tomatoes, and scallions. Drizzle with the vinaigrette dressing to taste and toss well.

Makes 4 to 6 servings

Spicy Soba Noodles and Vegetable Rolls

Soba Noodles

1	package (14 ounces) soba noodles
5	tablespoons sesame oil
	Pinch of sea salt
	Pinch of ground black pepper
1	onion, sliced

(continued)

2 carrots, julienned
2 cups shredded white cabbage
7 shiitake mushrooms
½ teaspoon Chinese five-spice powder (see note)
1½ cups Japanese Stock (see page 89)
¼ tablespoon chopped scallions
½ cup grated radishes

In a medium saucepan, cook the noodles according to the package directions for 6 to 7 minutes, or until al dente. Drain.

In a medium skillet, warm 3 tablespoons of the oil over medium heat. Add the noodles. Stir-fry for 2 to 3 minutes, stirring often. Add the salt and pepper. Reduce the heat to low and keep warm; do not overcook.

In a large skillet or wok, warm the remaining 2 tablespoons oil over medium heat. Add the onions, carrots, cabbage, mushrooms, five-spice powder, and stock. Stir-fry for 3 to 4 minutes. Add the noodles and toss well.

Transfer to a serving dish. Sprinkle with the scallions and radishes. Serve warm.

Makes 4 to 6 servings

Note: Chinese five-spice powder is available in most spice sections of supermarkets and in Asian markets.

Spinach Rolls with Sesame Sauce

Sauce

¼ cup + 1 tablespoon white sesame seeds
½ cup dashi
¼ cup + 2 tablespoons tamari
2 tablespoons mirin
1 tablespoon sugar
1½ tablespoons sake

Rolls

1¼   cups fresh spinach
4   large Chinese cabbage leaves
¼   cup + 1 tablespoon gomasio
     Sea salt

TO MAKE THE SAUCE: In a small heavy skillet, cook the sesame seeds over medium heat until golden brown. Keep moving the pan to avoid burning. Transfer the seeds to a grinding bowl and, using a pestle, grind them until flaky.

Add the dashi, tamari, mirin, sugar, and sake. Whisk together well and set aside.

TO MAKE THE ROLLS: Over medium-high heat, bring a medium pot of salted water to a boil. Add the spinach. Reduce the heat to medium and simmer for 2 minutes, stirring. Remove the spinach from the heat, reserve the cooking water, and run the spinach under cold water in a colander. Squeeze out the excess water.

In the same reserved cooking water, cook the cabbage for 2 to 3 minutes, or until just tender. Remove from the heat and run the cabbage under cold water to get a bright green color. Pat dry.

On a clean work surface, lay out the cabbage leaves. Sprinkle the leaves with ¼ cup of the gomasio and top each with the sauce and salt. Tightly roll each leaf, starting from stalk end. Squeeze out all excess water. Use a Japanese sushi rolling mat to make the job easier. With a sharp knife, cut each roll into four pieces. Sprinkle with the remaining 1 tablespoon gomasio.

Makes 4 to 6 servings

Chapter 8

AUTUMN

The EQUINOX ON SEPTEMBER 23 announces the harvesting season and the beginning of the yin energy, which will grow progressively stronger over the next six months. Temperatures drop and the colors of nature change dramatically, from dark greens to all hues of orange, red, and brown—nature is magnificent before its winter death. This is a time to stock your pantry with herbs, grains, and legumes for the cold months ahead; to stock up on fuel; to prepare your wardrobe for the rainy season and winter; and to repair your house against any leaks and drafts.

Autumn activities are mostly indoors, except for walks through the forests and the last hours spent in the garden protecting your plants from the cold to come. It is now that we read, write letters, and plan with family and friends in front of blazing fires.

Autumn is the season for fragrant kitchen smells—mulled wine, baking, and roasting chestnuts over open fires. In order to focus mentally and stimulate activity of the body, eat stews and lightly baked foods.

Autumn cooking methods: Simmering, baking, and sautéing—less water and more heat.

Autumn vegetables: Onions, squash, turnips, mushrooms, spinach, cauliflower, and sea vegetables.

Autumn grains: Rice, rye, bulgur, and cracked wheat.

Autumn fruits: Apples, limes, pears, chestnuts, hazelnuts, persimmons, pine nuts, and almonds.

Special autumn foods: Barley and barley malt, sesame seeds, rice syrup, millet, and soybean products (to combat dryness) such as tofu, tempeh, and soy milk.

Autumn herbs: Rosemary, ginger, burdock, and comfrey.

Suggested autumn body therapies: Dancing, doing yoga, breathing exercises, stretching, singing, humming, and sitting meditations.

Suggested autumn diet: Flavored foods, sauerkraut, umeboshi (pickled Japanese plums), rose hip tea, grilled sandwiches, couscous, millet pilaf, and adzuki beans.

LUNCH

Lentil Pâté Sandwiches

1½	cups lentils
2	tablespoons olive oil
1½	cups diced onions
½	teaspoon cumin seeds
5	cups water
1	teaspoon sea salt
2	teaspoons tamari
1	tablespoon garlic powder
1	teaspoon celery seeds
1	teaspoon mixed dried herbs
10	slices whole-wheat bread
	Soy mayonnaise
½	head lettuce, shredded
1	tomato, sliced
	Red onion rings

Preheat the broiler.

In a blender or food processor, or in a grinding bowl with a pestle, grind the lentils to a fine consistency.

In a large saucepan, warm the oil over medium heat. Add the onions and cumin seeds. Sauté for 5 minutes, or until the onions turn soft and the cumin seeds turn brown. Add the lentils, water, salt, tamari, garlic, celery seeds, and herbs. Bring to a boil and simmer, covered, for 1 hour.

Transfer the mixture to a loaf pan and chill for a few hours until firm, or overnight. When firm, invert the loaf pan onto a baking sheet and slice. Broil the pâté slices about 4" from the heat until the tops are lightly browned.

In the meantime, spread each of the bread slices with soy mayonnaise. Top half of the slices with the lettuce, tomatoes, grilled pâté, and onions. Cover each with another slice of bread.

Makes 5 servings

Warm Whole-Wheat Pitas with Beans

2	tablespoons sunflower oil
1	cup diced onions
1	cup scrubbed and diced white turnips
1	clove garlic, chopped
2	cups soaked and cooked black-eyed peas
1	tablespoon horseradish sauce
2	tablespoons chopped fresh parsley
4	pickling onions, chopped
2	cups vegetable stock
	Pinch of sea salt
	Pinch of ground black pepper
2	large pita breads
	Shredded lettuce

In a medium skillet, warm the oil over medium–low heat. Add the onions, turnips, and garlic. Cook for 10 minutes, stirring.

Stir in the peas, horseradish, parsley, and onions. Add the stock, salt, and pepper. Mix well. Cover and simmer for 20 minutes. Mash the mix with the back of a wooden spoon.

Cut the pitas in half to make a total of 4 small pockets. Place them in a microwave or preheated oven to warm. Split open the pitas and spread the bean mix inside. Top with the lettuce.

Makes 4 servings

Spicy Cabbage Rolls

2	teaspoons sunflower oil
½	teaspoon mustard seeds
½	teaspoon cumin seeds
½	teaspoon ground turmeric
1	medium green or white cabbage, shredded
1	teaspoon sea salt
2	teaspoons ground coriander
1	tablespoon lemon juice
4–6	large flour tortillas
	Olive oil
	Chopped fresh cilantro
	Hummus (optional), see page 71

In a large heavy skillet, warm the oil over medium heat. Add the mustard seeds and cumin seeds. When the seeds start to pop, add the turmeric, cabbage, salt, coriander, and lemon juice. Stir-fry for 8 to 10 minutes, mixing well.

Brush the tortillas with a little olive oil. Place them in a warm oven for 3 to 4 minutes to warm. Roll the cabbage mixture in the tortillas. Sprinkle with the cilantro. Spread with hummus (if using) for added flavor.

Makes 4 to 6 servings

Hot Potato Salad

¼ cup + 2 tablespoons sunflower oil
2 cloves garlic, crushed
1 tablespoon lemon juice
½ teaspoon coarse mustard
1 tablespoon balsamic vinegar
½ teaspoon honey
2 tablespoons chopped fresh parsley
2 tablespoons chopped black or green olives
6 scallions, sliced
20 small new potatoes, boiled or steamed (see note)

In a large bowl, combine the oil, garlic, lemon juice, mustard, vinegar, honey, parsley, olives, and scallions. Whisk together. Add the potatoes while still warm. Toss well. Let the salad stand for 30 minutes or more. Serve at room temperature.

Makes 4 to 6 servings

Note: The cooked new potatoes should be soft but not mushy.

Mediterranean Tofu on Toast

1 block firm tofu, drained and cubed
1 teaspoon dried rosemary
5 tablespoons olive oil
1 small red onion, sliced
2 cloves garlic, chopped
1 teaspoon sea salt
1 sweet red pepper, seeded and thinly sliced
1 sweet yellow pepper, seeded and thinly sliced
1 tablespoon capers
1 tablespoon chopped fresh basil
1 teaspoon ground black pepper
10 slices crusty herb bread

Preheat the broiler.

In a medium bowl, toss together the tofu, rosemary, and 2 tablespoons of the oil. Transfer the tofu to a baking sheet and broil about 4" under the heat, until slightly brown on all sides. Remove from the heat and set aside.

In a small skillet, warm 2 tablespoons of the oil over medium heat. Add the onions, garlic, and salt. Sauté until the onions turn translucent. Add the red and yellow peppers. Reduce the heat to low and cook for about 6 minutes, stirring often. Add the capers, basil, and black pepper. Cook for another 2 minutes. Remove from the heat.

Toast the herb bread slices lightly. Brush with the remaining 1 tablespoon oil. Arrange the tofu evenly over half of the bread slices. Top with the sautéed onions and peppers and cover with the remaining slices of bread.

Makes 5 servings

DINNER

STARTERS

Cabbage and White Bean Soup

2	cups white beans
4	tablespoons olive oil
1	cup chopped onions
3	cloves garlic, chopped
1	carrot, chopped
2	stalks celery, chopped
¼	cup chopped fresh parsley
¼	cup peeled, seeded, and chopped tomatoes
¼	cup caraway seeds

(continued)

2 cups shredded cabbage
3 cups vegetable stock
¼ cup cornmeal
Extra-virgin olive oil (optional)

In a large bowl of water, soak the beans overnight. Drain and cook according to the package directions or for 30 minutes in a pressure cooker. Drain, reserving the cooking liquid.

In a blender or food processor, puree 1 cup of the beans. Set aside.

In a large skillet, warm 3 tablespoons of the oil over medium heat. Add the onions, garlic, carrots, celery, and parsley. Sauté for 4 to 5 minutes. Add the tomatoes. Cook, stirring, for another 4 to 5 minutes. Remove from the heat.

In a large saucepan, warm the remaining 1 tablespoon oil over medium heat. Add the caraway seeds, shaking the pan so as not to burn them. Add the cabbage. Stir-fry for 3 to 4 minutes. Stir in the pureed beans and sautéed vegetables. Mix well. Cook for 2 minutes.

Add the stock and 1 cup of the reserved cooking liquid. Bring to a boil and simmer, covered, for 20 to 25 minutes, stirring occasionally. Stir in the remaining 1 cup beans. Add the cornmeal in a slow, thin stream, stirring constantly to avoid lumps. Simmer for 10 to 15 minutes more. Serve sprinkled with extra-virgin olive oil (if using).

Makes 4 to 6 servings

Mushrooms with Swiss Chard and Almonds

8 large button mushrooms
2 tablespoons olive oil
1 yellow onion, finely chopped
2 cloves garlic, chopped
4 cups chopped Swiss chard
¼ cup finely chopped roasted almonds
1 tablespoon lemon juice
¼ cup pesto

¼   cup dry bread crumbs
2   tablespoons chopped fresh parsley

Preheat the oven to 350°F. Lightly coat a baking sheet with nonstick cooking spray.

Wipe the mushrooms clean. Cut off the caps and lay them upside down on the baking sheet. Chop the mushroom stalks finely and set aside.

In a large skillet, warm the oil over medium heat. Add the onions. Cook until soft. Add the garlic, mushroom stalks, and Swiss chard. Mix well. Cook for 7 to 8 minutes. Add the almonds and mix well. Remove from the heat.

In a blender or food processor, combine the chard mixture, lemon juice, and pesto. Blend until smooth. Transfer the mixture into a large bowl. Stir in the bread crumbs and spoon carefully into the mushroom caps. Sprinkle with the parsley.

Bake for 15 to 18 minutes, or until the mushrooms are soft and juicy and the tops are crispy. Serve warm.

Makes 2 to 4 servings

Leeks au Gratin

¾   cup vegetable stock
10   baby leeks, halved lengthwise
2   tablespoons olive oil
¼   cup wine vinegar
¼   cup olive oil
2   tablespoons chopped shallots
1   tablespoon chopped fresh parsley
2   tablespoons chopped sweet red peppers
1   teaspoon mustard
    Pinch of sea salt
    Pinch of ground black pepper
2   tablespoons dry bread crumbs

Preheat the broiler.

In a large pot over medium–high heat, bring the stock to a boil. Add the leeks and blanch for 2 to 3 minutes. Drain well.

In a large skillet, warm the oil over medium heat. Add the leeks and cook for 4 minutes, stirring occasionally. Remove from the heat. Transfer the leeks to a deep baking dish.

In a medium bowl, combine the vinegar, oil, shallots, parsley, red peppers, mustard, salt, and black pepper. Whisk together. Pour the sauce over the leeks. Sprinkle with the bread crumbs.

Before serving, place the dish in the oven and broil 3" from the heat for 2 to 3 minutes, or until lightly browned. Serve warm.

Makes 4 to 6 servings

Cauliflower and Coconut Soup

3 cups vegetable stock
3 cups coconut milk
2 tablespoons chopped dried lemon grass (see note) or
   2 stalks lime leaves, chopped
2 tablespoons chopped fresh ginger
2 cloves garlic, sliced
2 peppercorns, crushed
1 small cauliflower, cut into florets
2 tablespoons soy sauce
1 teaspoon sugar
1 red chili pepper, seeded and chopped (optional), see
   note
1 tablespoon lime juice
   Chopped fresh cilantro
4 scallions, chopped

In a large saucepan, combine the stock, milk, lemon grass or lime leaves, ginger, garlic, peppercorns, cauliflower, soy sauce, sugar, and chili pepper (if using). Stir together well. Cook over medium heat, covered, for 20 minutes, or until the cauliflower is soft. Remove from the heat.

Stir in the lime juice. Serve sprinkled with the cilantro and scallions.

Makes 4 to 6 servings

Note: Fresh and dried lemon grass is available at Asian supermarkets.

Wear plastic gloves when handling the chili pepper.

Daikon Cakes in Oriental Sauce

1	large daikon, peeled and cut into small cubes
2½	cups rice flour
2	tablespoons whole-wheat flour
2	tablespoons water
3	tablespoons sesame oil
2	cloves garlic, chopped
2	tablespoons chopped fresh ginger
¼	cup soy sauce
¼	cup bean sprouts
4	scallions, chopped

In a blender or food processor, puree the daikon. Pour into a medium bowl. Add the rice and wheat flours and the water. Knead the mixture until it takes on a dough consistency.

Transfer the dough into a shallow cake pan and steam in a large steamer for 30 to 35 minutes. To check for readiness, insert a toothpick and see if it comes out clean. Remove from the heat and cool. Cut into small rectangles.

In a medium skillet, heat 1½ tablespoons of the oil over medium heat. Add the daikon cakes and fry until brown. Remove the cakes from the pan and place on a kitchen towel to drain excess oil.

Warm the remaining 1½ tablespoons oil in the skillet over medium heat. Add the garlic, ginger, soy sauce, and sprouts. Toss well. Add the fried daikon cakes and cook for 1 to 2 minutes, mixing well. Sprinkle with the scallions.

Makes 4 to 6 servings

ENTRÉES

Fried Tofu in Mediterranean Sauce

8	thick slices firm tofu, drained
	Sea salt
	Ground black pepper
6	tablespoons whole-wheat flour
6	tablespoons olive oil
2	cloves garlic, chopped
¼	cup chopped sun-dried tomatoes
2	tablespoons capers
10	artichoke quarters, marinated in oil
½	cup dry white wine or nonalcoholic white wine
¼	cup lemon juice
4	cups chopped spinach

Season the tofu slices with salt and pepper. Dredge them in the flour and shake off the excess.

In a large skillet, warm 4 tablespoons of the oil over medium-high heat. Add the tofu slices and fry in batches, turning them over once when lightly browned. Remove the tofu and keep warm in an oven.

In the same skillet, warm the remaining 2 tablespoons oil. Add the garlic, tomatoes, capers, artichokes, wine, and lemon juice. Bring to a boil and simmer for 6 to 8 minutes.

On a steaming rack over a pot of boiling water, steam the spinach for 5 minutes, or until bright green. Season lightly with salt and pepper.

Place a handful of spinach in the center of each of 4 dinner plates. Add 2 tofu slices on top of the spinach on each plate. Pour the sauce over the top of each. Serve warm.

Makes 4 servings

Vegetable Risotto with Mushroom and Watercress Casserole

Fennel Risotto

6	tablespoons olive oil
¼	cup chopped onions
¼	cup chopped celery
4	cups chopped fennel
2½	cups Arborio rice
½	cup dry white wine or nonalcoholic white wine
6½	cups vegetable stock
¼	cup chopped fresh parsley
1	tablespoon lemon juice
	Pinch of sea salt
	Pinch of ground black pepper

In a large skillet, warm 3 tablespoons of the oil over medium heat. Add the onions and celery. Sauté for 3 minutes, stirring often.

Add the fennel. Cook for 5 minutes until the fennel begins to brown. Reduce the heat to medium low. Add the rice and wine. Cook, stirring often, until the wine is absorbed. Add the stock gradually. Cook, stirring, for about 20 minutes, or until the rice is cooked al dente. Do not allow the rice to stick to the pan. Remove from the heat. Sprinkle with the parsley, lemon juice, salt, and pepper. Serve warm.

Makes 4 to 6 servings

Mushroom and Watercress Bake

4	tablespoons olive oil
2	cups halved mushrooms
1	tablespoon lemon juice
1	tablespoon whole-meal flour

(continued)

1   teaspoon dry mustard
¾   cup soy milk
2   bunches watercress
1   tablespoon chopped fresh parsley
    Pinch of sea salt
    Pinch of ground black pepper

Preheat the oven to 375°F.

In a medium skillet, warm 2 tablespoons of the oil over medium heat. Add the mushrooms. Cook for 2 minutes. Pour in the lemon juice. Cook until the juice is absorbed. Remove from the heat. Using a slotted spoon, transfer the mushrooms to a baking dish. Set aside.

In a medium saucepan, warm the remaining 2 tablespoons oil. Add the flour and mustard. Cook, stirring continuously, for 3 to 4 minutes. Remove from the heat. Add the milk, stirring well to avoid lumps. Return to the burner and simmer for 4 minutes. Fold in the watercress and allow to wilt. Cook for about 2 minutes more.

Pour the watercress sauce over the mushrooms in the baking dish. Bake for 20 minutes. Turn the oven to broil for the last 5 minutes to brown. Sprinkle with the parsley, salt, and pepper.

Makes 4 to 6 servings

Millet Pilaf with Aviyal

Herbed Millet Pilaf

2   tablespoons olive oil
1   teaspoon cumin seeds
1   large onion, chopped
2   cloves garlic, chopped
1   teaspoon grated fresh ginger
½   teaspoon ground coriander
2   stalks celery, chopped
1   carrot, grated

1   cup dried millet
    About 4 cups vegetable stock
½   teaspoon sea salt
2   tablespoons chopped fresh cilantro
1   tablespoon chopped fresh parsley
1   tablespoon pine nuts
1   tablespoon currants

In a large heavy skillet, warm the oil over medium heat. Add the cumin seeds, onions, garlic, ginger, and coriander. Cook, stirring well, for 5 to 7 minutes. Add the celery and carrots. Cook for 6 to 8 minutes, or until the onions are tender.

Stir in the millet, stock, and salt. Bring to a boil. Cover and simmer over low heat for 30 to 40 minutes. If needed, add extra stock before simmering millet.

When done cooking, fluff the millet with a fork. Stir in the cilantro, parsley, nuts, and currants. Serve warm.

Makes 4 to 6 servings

Aviyal

1   cup dry, shredded coconut
¾   cup water
1   tablespoon olive oil
1   cup sliced onions
2   teaspoons chopped fresh ginger
3   cloves garlic, chopped
2   teaspoons ground coriander
2   teaspoons ground turmeric
1   tablespoon garam masala powder (optional)
    Pinch of sea salt
½   cup green beans, halved
2   carrots, sliced
1   cup diced squash

(continued)

                2   cups broccoli florets
                1   red chili pepper, seeded and chopped (see note)

   In a blender or food processor, combine the coconut and water.
Blend until smooth.

   In a medium heavy skillet, warm the oil over medium heat. Add the
onions, ginger, and garlic. Sauté until lightly browned. Add the coriander,
turmeric, garam masala, and salt. Mix well. Cook for 2 to 3 minutes more.

   Add the beans, carrots, squash, and broccoli. Cook for 2 to 3 minutes,
stirring often. Pour in the coconut mixture and bring to a boil. Cover
and simmer for 8 minutes. Stir in the chili pepper.

Makes 4 to 6 servings

Note: Wear plastic gloves when handling the chili pepper.

Kasha, Spinach, and Pasta with Steamed Beets

Kasha and Spinach with Pasta

                2   cups kasha
                1   bay leaf
               4¾   cups vegetable stock
                ½   packet (7 ounces) soba noodles
                2   tablespoons olive oil
                1   cup sliced onions
                2   cups halved mushrooms
                2   cloves garlic, chopped
                1   tablespoon chopped fresh thyme
                1   tablespoon chopped fresh rosemary
                1   tablespoon chopped fresh sage
                1   tablespoon whole-wheat flour
                4   cups chopped spinach
                ½   teaspoon freshly grated nutmeg
                     Nori flakes

Add the kasha to a large heavy-bottomed saucepan, and briefly cook over medium-high heat, stirring constantly. Add the bay leaf and 4 cups of the stock. Bring to a boil. Reduce the heat to medium and simmer, covered, for 20 minutes, or until soft, stirring once or twice.

In a medium pot of salted boiling water, cook the noodles according to the package directions. Remove from the heat and set aside.

In a large skillet, warm the oil over medium heat. Add the onions. Sauté for 1 to 2 minutes. Add the mushrooms, garlic, thyme, rosemary, and sage. Stir well for 2 minutes. Add the flour. Sauté, stirring, until the flour is lightly browned. By handfuls, add the spinach until it wilts. Sprinkle the nutmeg over the top. Reduce the heat to low and cook for 3 to 5 minutes. Add the remaining ¾ cup stock and bring to a boil. Whisk together well. Cook until the sauce reduces in volume by half.

Transfer the soba noodles and kasha, removing the bay leaf, onto a serving platter. Stir together well and ladle the mushroom sauce over top. Toss well. Sprinkle with the nori flakes.

Makes 4 to 6 servings

Steamed Beets

2–3 raw beets, sliced
2 tablespoons olive oil
2 tablespoons lemon juice
1 teaspoon ground ginger
2 teaspoons chopped fresh parsley
2 teaspoons chopped walnuts
1 teaspoon balsamic vinegar
Pinch of sea salt
Pinch of ground black pepper

On a steaming rack over a pot of boiling water, steam the beets for 25 to 30 minutes, or until tender.

(continued)

In a small bowl, combine the oil, lemon juice, ginger, parsley, nuts, vinegar, salt, and pepper. Whisk together well.

Arrange the beets on a serving platter and pour the dressing over top. Serve warm.

Makes 4 to 6 servings

Chickpea-Potato Casserole with Tangy Arugula Salad

Chickpea and Potato Bake

2	cups peeled whole pearl onions
4	tablespoons olive oil
3	sprigs of thyme
½	cup coarsely chopped carrots
½	cup coarsely chopped celery
½	cup coarsely chopped onions
1	bay leaf
2	cups halved mushrooms
1	clove garlic, chopped
	Pinch of sea salt
	Pinch of ground black pepper
1½	cups dry white wine or nonalcoholic white wine
4	cups diced potatoes
2	cups cooked chickpeas
¼	cup pitted green olives
1	lemon, sliced

Preheat the oven to 350°F.

Wrap the pearl onions in foil with 2 tablespoons of the oil and 2 sprigs of the thyme. Bake for 45 minutes.

In a large skillet, warm the remaining 2 tablespoons oil over medium heat. Add the carrots, celery, onions, and bay leaf. Sauté for 6 to 8 minutes, or until lightly browned. Add the mushrooms, garlic, remaining sprig of thyme, salt, and pepper. Sauté, stirring often, for another 6 minutes, or until the mushrooms turn soft. Pour the wine over the vegetables. Continue cooking over medium heat for another 5 to 6 minutes, allowing the wine to evaporate. Remove from the heat.

In a baking dish, combine the cooked vegetables with the potatoes and chickpeas. Cover the dish with foil and cook in the oven for 20 to 25 minutes. Remove the foil. Continue cooking until mixture is lightly browned on top. When done, remove from the heat. Top with the olives, baked onions, and lemon slices.

Makes 4 to 6 servings

Arugula and Tomato Salad

1	whole-wheat focaccia, cubed
½	cup Lemon Vinaigrette (see page 83)
3	cups chopped arugula
1	cup thinly sliced onions
2	large tomatoes, chopped

In a large bowl, combine the focaccia cubes with ¼ cup of the vinaigrette. Toss together and set aside for a few minutes.

Add the arugula, onions, and tomatoes. Drizzle with the remaining ¼ cup vinaigrette. Toss well and serve.

Makes 4 to 6 servings

Chapter 9

WINTER

HE SOLSTICE ON DECEMBER 21, our longest night, marks the beginning of winter. Yin energy is now at its most potent—everything that is inner, mysterious, and dark is emphasized. We dress in warm clothing and limit outdoor activities to fun-packed games and sports in the snow, like skiing, snowshoeing, and sledding down snow-covered hills, and then we relieve the day's outdoor adventures in front of the fireplace. This is the time when animals sleep and the world outside is quiet. It is a time for deep meditation, contemplation, and reflection before action, and a time to rest and store physical energy—many people put on a little weight during these cold months.

We keep our houses warm by keeping constant, even temperatures (not sudden heats and colds); we wear warmer clothes and keep our feet warm. This is also the time for hot beverages and stews to prevent chills from ailing us. Winter is a very feminine time—one of understanding, wisdom, and inner strength.

To attune with winter, eat wholesome grains, increase fat intake, and cook your meals.

Winter cooking methods: Cook longer at lower temperatures with less water. Boiling, steaming, baking, and light frying.

Winter vegetables: Carrots, turnips, broccoli, potatoes, kale, onions, cabbage, and celery.

Winter grains: Buckwheat, kasha (buckwheat groats), amaranth, millet, and rice.

Winter fruits: Apples, oranges, and dried fruits.

Special winter foods: Tofu, goat's cheese, miso, and legumes for protein; licorice, chicory, and horsetail for a bitter taste; and soy sauce, sea vegetables, and barley for a salty taste.

Winter herbs: Marshmallow root, nettle, and herbal teas.

Suggested winter body therapies: Choose a warm spot to exercise in at home or wear extra layers of clothing when coming out of the gym. Yoga, stretching, deep and still meditations, aromatherapy, reiki, deep tissue massage, and shiatsu.

Suggested winter diet: Soups, bakes, soba noodles, lentil nut loaf, fried rice, and miso soup.

LUNCH

One-Pot Noodles

1	package udon noodles
1	cup Japanese Stock (see page 89)
1	teaspoon tamari
2	tablespoons mustard
1	teaspoon mirin
8–10	shiitake mushroom caps, soaked and chopped
1	carrot, julienned
6	water chestnuts
1	cup finely chopped pumpkin

(continued)

1   cup shredded cabbage
4   scallions, sliced
2   tablespoons sesame oil

Cook the noodles according to the package directions. Drain and rinse under cold water. Keep the noodles in a large bowl filled with cold water to prevent them from sticking together.

In a large saucepan, combine the stock, tamari, mustard, and mirin. Warm, stirring, over medium heat. One by one, add the mushrooms, carrots, water chestnuts, and pumpkin. Stir well. Add the cabbage and scallions. Cook for 6 to 8 minutes.

Drain the noodles. Toss with the oil and add to the stock. Simmer until heated through. Serve with additional tamari and mustard.

Makes 4 to 6 servings

Molletes Mexican-Style

1   loaf French or Italian bread
2   tablespoons olive oil
1   teaspoon cumin seeds
½   cup chopped onions
1½ teaspoons ground coriander
    Pinch of sea salt
    Pinch of ground black pepper
1   cup coarsely mashed cooked red or black beans
2–4 tablespoons chopped tomatoes
½   cup nondairy cheese (optional)

Preheat the broiler.

Slice the bread into 4 sections across and then slice each piece in half lengthwise. Scoop out some bread from each piece, making 8 cradles.

In a medium skillet, warm the oil over medium heat. Add the cumin seeds. Cook until they start to change color. Add the onions, coriander, salt, and pepper. Sauté until the onions turn light brown. Stir in the beans and tomatoes. Cook for 6 to 8 minutes, stirring often. Remove from the heat.

Spoon the bean mixture into the bread cradles. Top with the cheese (if using). Place the bread on a baking sheet in the oven. Broil until the tops turn light brown. Serve warm.

Makes 4 to 6 servings

Nut Burgers

2	tablespoons olive oil
1	cup chopped onions
1	clove garlic, crushed
1	teaspoon ground coriander
1	teaspoon dry mustard
¼	cup flour
½	cup water or vegetable stock
2	cups chopped mixed nuts
1	cup fresh bread crumbs
2	cups coarsely grated carrots
1	tablespoon chopped fresh parsley
1	tablespoon lemon juice

Preheat the oven to 350°F. Lightly coat a baking sheet with nonstick cooking spray.

In a large skillet, warm the oil over medium heat. Add the onions, garlic, coriander, and mustard. Sauté until the onions turn tender. Stir in the flour. Cook, stirring, for 2 to 3 minutes more.

In a slow, steady stream, pour in the water or stock. Mix well and bring to a boil. Remove from the heat. Stir in the nuts, bread crumbs, carrots, parsley, and lemon juice. Let the mixture stand until cold.

Using your hands, shape the mixture into round burger patties. Place them on the prepared baking sheet.

Bake for about 25 minutes, turning the patties over after 15 minutes to cook evenly. Serve warm or at room temperature with a raw salad.

Makes 4 to 6 servings

Fried Fennel Sandwiches

          2   bulbs fennel, cut into 2"-thick slices
          ¼   cup whole-wheat flour
          ¼   cup + 2 tablespoons olive oil
          1   loaf crusty Italian bread
          1   tomato, sliced
              Sea salt
              Ground black pepper

Preheat the broiler.

In a medium pot of boiling water, boil the fennel for 3 to 4 minutes. Drain well. Dredge the fennel slices in the flour. Shake off the excess flour and set aside.

In a large skillet, warm ¼ cup of the oil over high heat. Add the fennel slices and fry until golden brown on all sides. Remove from the heat and drain the slices on paper towels.

Slice the bread lengthwise and brush with the remaining 2 tablespoons oil. Top with the fennel and tomato. Place the bread on a baking sheet.

Broil until the tomatoes are charred. Season with the salt and pepper.

Makes 4 to 6 servings

Eggplant and Hummus Sandwiches

          1   large eggplant, sliced
              Sea salt
          6   tablespoons olive oil
          1   clove garlic, chopped
          2   tablespoons chopped fresh parsley
          1   tablespoon chopped fresh basil
          1   tablespoon lemon juice
              Ground black pepper
          1   tablespoon balsamic vinegar

10   slices whole–wheat bread
¼   cup + 1 tablespoon Hummus (see page 71)

Place the eggplant in a colander and sprinkle with salt. Let stand for 30 minutes. Rinse and drain well, patting dry.

In a large skillet, warm the oil over medium–high heat. Add the eggplant and garlic. Sauté until lightly browned on both sides. Remove with a slotted spoon and place the eggplant on paper towels to drain excess oil. Season with the parsley, basil, lemon juice, salt, pepper, and vinegar.

Toast the bread slices and spread the hummus lightly on each. Place two slices of eggplant on each slice of bread and top with another slice of bread.

Makes 5 servings

DINNER

STARTERS

Fava Bean Bruschetta

2½   cups fava beans, cooked
¼   cup chopped sun–dried tomatoes
3   cloves garlic, chopped
    Sea salt
    Ground black pepper
1   tablespoon olive oil

(continued)

         2   cups broccoli florets
         2   tablespoons olive oil
         4   slices (1½" thick) Italian or French bread
             Toasted sesame seeds

In a blender or food processor, combine the beans, tomatoes, 1 clove of the garlic, salt, and pepper. Blend together to make a coarse puree.

In a medium skillet, warm the oil over medium heat. Add the broccoli and the remaining 2 cloves garlic. Sauté until the broccoli is crisp-tender.

Lightly toast the bread slices. Spread the bean mixture on each slice and top with the broccoli. Serve warm, sprinkled with the sesame seeds.

Makes 4 servings

Carrot-Parsnip Cakes
with Shallot-Plum Sauce

Cakes

         3   carrots, chopped
         3   parsnips, chopped
         2   tablespoons olive oil
             Chopped fresh parsley
             Pinch of sea salt
             Pinch of ground black pepper
         1   cup self-rising flour

Sauce

         1   tablespoon olive oil
         3   shallots
         2   cloves garlic, chopped
         ¼   cup plum sauce (see note)
         2   tablespoons water
         ⅛   red chili pepper, chopped (see note)
             Soy sauce

Preheat the broiler.

TO MAKE THE CAKES: In a large pot of boiling water, cook the carrots and parsnips for 15 minutes, or until tender. Drain and mash well. Add the oil, parsley, salt, and pepper. Mix well. Set aside to cool.

Spread the flour onto a clean work surface. Pour the vegetable mixture on top and work in the flour. Knead well. Let stand until ready to cook.

Roll out the dough and cut into 1"-thick round cakes. Place the cakes on a baking sheet and cook in the oven for 3 to 4 minutes on each side.

TO MAKE THE SAUCE: In a small skillet, warm the oil over medium heat. Add the shallots and garlic. Sauté for 5 minutes, or until the shallots soften. Remove from the heat.

In a small bowl, combine the shallots and garlic with the plum sauce, water, chili pepper, and soy sauce. Whisk together. Serve as a dipping sauce for the cakes.

Makes 4 to 6 servings

Note: Plum sauce, also known as hoisin or Peking sauce, is available in most supermarkets and in Asian markets.

Wear plastic gloves when handling the chili pepper.

Lentil Parcels with Cilantro Dipping Sauce

Parcels

4	tablespoons olive oil
2	teaspoons mustard seeds
8	scallions, chopped
2	cups finely chopped spinach
2	teaspoons grated fresh ginger
½	teaspoon freshly grated or ground nutmeg
1	cup red lentils, cooked
	Pinch of sea salt
	Pinch of ground black pepper

(continued)

10–15	wonton wrappers (see note)
1	egg, lightly beaten

Sauce

2	cups chopped fresh cilantro
¼	cup lemon juice
¼	cup unsweetened shredded coconut
2	tablespoons grated fresh ginger
1	teaspoon honey
1	teaspoon sea salt
1	teaspoon ground black pepper

TO MAKE THE PARCELS: In a large skillet, warm 2 tablespoons of the oil over medium heat. Add the mustard seeds. Sauté the seeds until they start to pop then add the scallions. Cook, stirring well, for another 2 minutes.

In small handfuls, stir in the spinach. Stir in the ginger and nutmeg. Mix well. Cook until the spinach has wilted. Stir in the lentils, salt, and pepper. Cook for 4 to 5 minutes. Remove from the heat and cool.

Place a teaspoon of the lentil mixture into the center of each wonton wrapper. Brush the edges with the egg. Bring up two opposite points of the wrapper over the filling and pinch them together in the center. Bring the remaining opposite points to the center and pinch together. Pinch all the edges together to seal.

Steam in a steamer for 4 to 7 minutes, or until firm but still tender.

TO MAKE THE SAUCE: In a blender or food processor, combine the cilantro, lemon juice, coconut, ginger, honey, salt, and pepper. Blend together until smooth. If sauce seems too thick, add a little water until you get the desired consistency.

Pour the sauce into individual dipping bowls and serve with the lentil parcels.

Makes 4 to 6 servings

Note: Wonton wrappers are sold frozen in Asian markets and in many supermarkets.

Celeriac Soup with Grilled Onions

Soup

2	tablespoons olive oil
5	leeks, sliced (white part only)
1	medium bulb fennel, sliced
½	teaspoon fennel seeds
1	teaspoon celery seeds
2	cloves garlic, crushed
1	teaspoon sea salt
2	tablespoons chopped fresh parsley
	About 3 cups vegetable stock
2	tablespoons chopped fennel leaves (the inner feathery green part)
1	stalk celery, sliced

Grilled Onions

1	large sweet onion, peeled and finely sliced
1	tablespoon olive oil

Preheat the broiler.

TO MAKE THE SOUP: In a large saucepan, warm the oil over medium heat. Add the leeks. Sauté until they become brighter in color. Add the sliced fennel, fennel and celery seeds, garlic, salt, and parsley. Cook, stirring often, for 4 to 5 minutes.

Add 2 cups of the stock, the fennel leaves, and celery. Cover and simmer for 20 minutes. Check occasionally to see if water is needed while simmering. Add 1 cup more of the stock. Cover and cook for another 15 minutes. Remove from the heat and set aside to cool.

TO MAKE THE GRILLED ONIONS: In a small bowl, toss the onions and oil until the onions are well-coated. Transfer to a baking sheet and place in the oven. Broil, turning often, until just lightly browned.

(continued)

Pour the soup into a blender or food processor. Blend until smooth. If the soup is too thick, add more stock. Heat thoroughly. Serve topped with the onions.

Makes 4 to 6 servings

Split-Pea Soup

2	tablespoons olive oil
1	cup chopped onions
3	cloves garlic, crushed
2	stalks celery, chopped
1	cup chopped carrots
1	small parsnip, finely chopped
1	teaspoon sea salt
¼	teaspoon ground nutmeg
1	cup split peas, soaked for 8 to 10 hours and drained
	About 6 cups vegetable stock
⅛	teaspoon ground black pepper
2	tablespoons chopped fresh cilantro
¼	cup chopped fresh parsley

In a large saucepan, warm the oil over medium heat. Add the onions and garlic. Sauté until the onions soften. Add the celery, carrots, parsnips, salt, and nutmeg. Cook, stirring well, until the vegetables turn slightly brown. Stir in the peas, stock, and pepper. Bring to a boil. Cover and simmer for about 1½ hours. If required, add more stock or water to thin the soup. Remove from the heat and cool.

In a blender or food processor, puree about one-quarter of the soup. Return to the saucepan and reheat.

Before serving, sprinkle with the cilantro and parsley.

Makes 4 to 6 servings

ENTRÉES

Penne Bake with Broccoli, Sun-Dried Tomatoes, and Capers

This dish is excellent served warm over a bed of winter greens or steamed Swiss chard.

1	package (16 ounces) penne pasta
4	tablespoons olive oil
¼	cup dried bread crumbs
3	cloves garlic, chopped
1	cup chopped purple broccoli, steamed
¼	cup chopped sun-dried tomatoes
2	tablespoons capers
1	teaspoon chopped fresh rosemary
	Sea salt
	Ground black pepper
2	tablespoons chopped fresh parsley
2	tablespoons chopped fresh basil

In a large pot of boiling, salted water, cook the pasta according to the package directions until al dente.

In a large skillet, warm 2 tablespoons of the oil over low heat. Stir in the bread crumbs. Cook, stirring, until golden brown.

Add the garlic. Sauté for a few seconds before adding the broccoli, tomatoes, capers, and rosemary. Stir and cook until heated well. Season with salt and pepper.

Drain the pasta and add to the skillet. Stir in the remaining 2 tablespoons oil, the parsley, and basil. Mix well.

Makes 4 to 6 servings

Winter Vegetables in Oriental Sauce

Vegetables

¼	cup olive oil
3	parsnips, cubed
2	yams or sweet potatoes, cubed
10–12	brussels sprouts, with hard leaves removed
3	carrots, coarsely chopped

Sauce

2	tablespoons olive oil
1	cup chopped onions
1	tablespoon grated fresh ginger
1	cup black-eyed peas, cooked and slightly mashed
	Pinch of sea salt
	Pinch of ground black pepper
2	cups chopped tomatoes
4	tablespoons chopped fresh cilantro
2	cups coconut milk
1	tablespoon soy sauce (optional)

TO PREPARE THE VEGETABLES: Preheat the oven to 350°F.

In a medium bowl, combine the oil, parsnips, and yams or sweet potatoes. Toss until the vegetables are well-coated and place in a baking dish. Cook in the oven for 30 minutes, or until soft and golden.

In a medium pot of boiling, salted water, cook the brussels sprouts for 2 to 3 minutes, or until bright in color. Remove the brussels sprouts from the pot and set aside. On a steaming rack set over the pot of boiling water, steam the carrots for 6 to 20 minutes, or until crisp-tender.

TO MAKE THE SAUCE: In a large heavy saucepan, warm the oil over medium heat. Add the onions and ginger. Sauté until lightly brown. Add the peas, salt, and pepper. Mix well. Stir in the tomatoes and cook, stirring, for 5 to 6 minutes. Add 2 tablespoons of the cilantro, the coconut milk, and soy sauce (if using). Stir well. Cover and simmer for 5 to 6 minutes. Remove from the heat and stir in the remaining 2 tablespoons cilantro.

Add all the vegetables to the saucepan and mix well over low heat. Cook for 6 to 8 minutes or until heated thoroughly.

Makes 4 to 6 servings

Cornbread with Sautéed Vegetables

Cornbread

1	cup cornmeal
½	cup barley flour
½	cup oat flour
½	teaspoon sea salt
1	teaspoon baking powder
2	cups soy milk
1	tablespoon apple butter or maple syrup

Preheat the oven to 350°F. Lightly coat a square 8" × 8" baking pan with nonstick cooking spray.

Over a large bowl, sift together the cornmeal, barley and oat flours, salt, and baking powder. Stir in the milk and apple butter or maple syrup. Mix well. Pour the mixture into the prepared pan and let stand for 1 hour.

Bake for 40 to 45 minutes. Remove from the oven and cool slightly on a wire rack before slicing. The cornbread squares can be brushed with olive oil and broiled briefly before serving.

Makes 4 to 6 servings

Sautéed Vegetables

2	tablespoons sesame oil
½	cup leeks, julienned

(continued)

½	cup sliced onions
1	clove garlic, peeled
6	shiitake mushrooms, soaked, drained, and thinly sliced
1	cup cauliflower florets
1	cup finely sliced squash
1	cup bean sprouts
1	cup snow peas
1	teaspoon ground coriander
1	tablespoon tamari
1	teaspoon sugar

In a wok or large skillet, warm the oil over medium heat. Add the leeks, onions, and garlic. Sauté until the onions are slightly soft, then discard the garlic. Stir in the mushrooms, cauliflower, and squash. Toss well and sauté for 5 to 8 minutes. Add the sprouts and snow peas. Cook for another 2 minutes. Stir in the coriander, tamari, and sugar. Mix well.

Makes 4 to 6 servings

Cauliflower Béchamel with Baked Potatoes

Cauliflower in Béchamel Sauce

Sauce

1	quart soy milk
7	mushrooms, chopped
½	pumpkin, diced
2	stalks celery, chopped
1	leek, chopped
1	large onion, chopped
4	cloves garlic, chopped
2	bay leaves
	Pinch of nutmeg
1	tablespoon oil

¼ cup flour
Chopped fresh herbs
Pinch of sea salt
Pinch of ground black pepper

Cauliflower

1 small head cauliflower, chopped into florets
7 whole shallots
Chopped fresh parsley

To make the sauce: In a large saucepan, combine the milk, mushrooms, pumpkin, celery, leeks, onions, garlic, bay leaves, and nutmeg. Mix well. Simmer, stirring occasionally, over low heat for 30 minutes.

In another large saucepan, warm the oil over low heat. Stir in the flour. Cook, stirring often, for a few minutes. Strain the milk through a sieve and add to the flour, pouring slowly in a thin stream and stirring constantly. Cook, whisking together vigorously, until the sauce thickens. Stir in the herbs, salt, and pepper. Keep warm over a double boiler.

To make the cauliflower: Preheat the broiler.

On a steaming rack over a large pot of boiling water, steam the cauliflower and shallots for about 10 minutes, or until soft but not mushy.

Transfer into a baking dish. Pour the sauce over the cauliflower and shallots. Cook in the oven until lightly browned. Sprinkle with the parsley and serve warm.

Makes 4 to 6 servings

Herbed Baked Potatoes

6 large potatoes
2 tablespoons olive oil
2–3 sprigs fresh rosemary
6 cloves garlic, peeled

Preheat the oven to 350°F.

In a large pot of boiling, salted water, cook the potatoes for 8 to 10 minutes. Remove from the heat and set aside until cool enough to handle. Peel and cut into quarters.

Place the potatoes in a baking dish. Add the oil, rosemary, and garlic. Stir together until well-mixed. Bake for 25 to 30 minutes, or until brown.

Makes 4 to 6 servings

Vegetable Rösti with Pan-Fried Artichokes and Mushrooms

Potato and Zucchini Rösti

> 3   tablespoons olive oil
> 1   cup chopped onions
> 4–5 medium potatoes, peeled and coarsely grated
> 2   medium zucchini, coarsely grated
> ¼   cup chopped fresh parsley
>   Pinch of sea salt
>   Pinch of ground black pepper

In a large skillet, warm 1 tablespoon of the oil over medium heat. Add the onions. Sauté until the onions turn soft.

In a medium bowl, combine the onions, potatoes, and zucchini. Season with the parsley, salt, and pepper. Mix well.

Heat the remaining 2 tablespoons oil in the skillet. Add the potato mixture and cook, stirring occasionally, for 6 to 8 minutes. Using a spatula, flatten the mixture into a cake form. Cook for 8 to 10 minutes, or until well-browned. Serve hot, cut into wedges.

Makes 4 to 6 servings

Sautéed Artichokes and Mushrooms

6 tablespoons olive oil
3 cups sliced mushrooms
8 artichoke hearts, cooked and sliced
2 shallots, chopped
2 cloves garlic, crushed
2 tablespoons capers
2 tablespoons chopped fresh chervil
2 tablespoons chopped fresh parsley
½ cup chopped fresh basil
2 tablespoons mustard
Pinch of sea salt
Pinch of ground black pepper
1 medium tomato, sliced
Lemon juice

Preheat the broiler. Coat a shallow baking dish with nonstick cooking spray.

In a large skillet, warm 2 tablespoons of the oil over medium heat. Add the mushrooms, artichokes, and shallots. Sauté until golden. Remove from the skillet and keep warm.

Using a mortar and pestle or a food processor, grind the garlic, capers, chervil, parsley, and basil into a fine paste. Add the mustard, salt, pepper, and remaining 4 tablespoons oil. Whisk together well. Pour this sauce over the sautéed vegetables.

Transfer the mixture into the prepared baking dish, alternating layers with the tomato slices. Sprinkle a little lemon juice over the top. Broil for 10 to 15 minutes, or until browned.

Makes 4 to 6 servings

Part III

HARMONY BETWEEN BODY AND SPIRIT

Chapter 10

MEDITATION—THE ART OF INNER GARDENING

I N THE WEST, WE DO NOT practice meditation because we too readily dismiss it as being part and parcel of a lifestyle that is impossible to integrate with our own. Ascetic spirituality seems at odds with the everyday hustle and bustle of family, work, and the need to sustain a social life. We have notions that meditation is something that Indian sadhus or Zen monks practice in faraway lands where they are cloistered away from the world and its demands. And yet it is today that we need meditation, perhaps far more than in the times of Buddha or the other venerable Indian masters who taught the importance of silence and of looking at the world as though into a mirror that reflects back images of ourselves.

The Bible tells us that paradise is a garden. We may deduce that a good path to that paradise is the creation of our own gardens, not just physical places to grace our homes but an inner space, a sanctuary where we find enchantment and regeneration that is entirely our own. This is a place where we come to take a rest from all those hooks that anchor us to life—stress, grief, worry, anger, frustration—and allow them to be dissolved and transformed into more positive, workable energy patterns. The garden is also the magical seat where feelings that give us wings to fly through life—joy, compassion, enthusiasm, love, friendship—are enhanced and valued. And, lastly, the garden is also a place of silence and stillness, where only the pulsing of our beings is felt. If we have never had any experience of soul, this is where the meeting is finally going to happen. Meditation is the art of inner gardening.

Sitting silently,

Doing nothing,

Spring comes,

And the grass grows by itself.
—Osho, from *Talks on Zen*

Creating the Inner Garden

Meditation is very simple; all you need is the wish to begin a wondrous journey, a cushion to sit on, and a private place where you feel safe and relaxed. Visit the rooms in your home and find a spot where you feel that you can begin creating the inner garden. It may be a room that is not used very frequently, somewhere you can retire to and feel that you can be alone and silent. This spot may change at different times of the year—you may be drawn to meditate outdoors during late spring and summer but prefer a warmer spot in winter.

Although initially this may be difficult, it is best to meditate every day for 45 minutes to 1 hour. Entering the inner garden is like passing through a mystical gate, and things are not the same on the other side, thus it takes a little time to adjust to the different climate. Be patient—you will soon begin to reap the benefits from your hour alone cultivating the inner garden.

The best times for meditation are early morning and in the evening at sunset; these are the hours when consciousness is most transparent. If you meditate between 6:00 and 7:00 A.M. and between 7:00 and 8:00 P.M., you will find it easier to be completely immersed in the silence of your being. Dawn and dusk are especially magical times, when the quality of light is between day and night, suffusing the world with softness. It is very beautiful to be still when everything around is slowly stirring to awaken or settling to rest.

Some simple, yet powerful, meditations that anyone can practice are suggested here. Read all the meditations in the following sections then choose the one that most appeals to you. Practice this meditation every day for a minimum of three weeks and up to three months. If you find it helpful, keep a meditation journal and observe the changes as they unfold. You may want to start your meditation course on a particular day, such as on the new moon, full moon, or at an equinox. These are cosmically charged times and the energies whirling around you will help to focus your attention on the meditative process. Meditation is not a heroic act; it is about the deep, mysterious stirrings of your being. You may be disappointed at first and feel that nothing is happening to you. Do not as a consequence become obsessed and practice as though you were muscle building. Be patient. Be still. Know that the changes that will happen may not be great, but they will be profound and will alter the quality of other areas of your life.

The following meditations were devised or adapted from ancient methods by Osho, an enlightened master who has been working with all possibilities to help humanity develop and raise consciousness. His established commune in Pune, India, and his many centers all over the world help thousands to experience meditation and transformation. His teachings have influenced millions of people of all ages and from all walks of life.

Vipassana

Find a comfortable place to sit for 45 minutes to an hour. It helps to sit at the same time and in the same place every day, and it doesn't have to be a silent place. Experiment until you find the situation in which you feel best. You can sit once or twice a day, but don't meditate for at least an hour after eating or before sleeping.

It's important to sit with your back and head straight. Your eyes should be closed and your body as still as possible. A meditation bench can help, or a straight-backed chair or any arrangement of cushions.

There is no special breathing technique; ordinary, natural breathing is fine. Vipassana is based on the awareness of the breath, so the rise and fall of each breath should be watched, wherever the sensation is felt most clearly—in the nose or in the area of the stomach or solar plexus.

Vipassana is not concentration, and it is not an objective to remain watching the breathing for a whole hour. When thoughts, feelings, or sensations arise, or when you become aware of sounds, smells, and breezes, simply allow your attention to go to them. Whatever comes up can be watched as clouds passing in the sky—you neither cling nor reject. Whenever there is a choice of what to watch, return to your awareness of breathing.

Remember, nothing special is meant to happen. There is neither success nor failure—nor is there any improvement. There is nothing to figure out or analyze, but insights may come about anything. Questions and problems may be just seen as mysteries to be enjoyed.

—Osho, from *The Revolution*

Nadabrahma

Nadabrahma is an old Tibetan technique that was originally done in the early hours of the morning. It can be done at any time of the day, alone or with others, but you should begin with an empty stomach and remain inactive for at least 15 minutes afterward. The meditation lasts an hour and there are three stages. (For a copy of the Nadabrahma meditation tape, which has different music announcing each stage of the meditation, write to one of the companies listed on page 230.)

First stage: 30 minutes. Sit in a relaxed position with your eyes closed and lips together. Start humming, loudly enough to be heard by others and to create a vibration throughout your body. You can visualize a hollow tube or an empty vessel filled only with the vibration of the humming. A point will come when the humming continues by itself and you become the listener. There is no special breathing, and you can alter the pitch of the humming or move your body smoothly and slowly if you feel like it.

Second stage: 15 minutes. The second stage is divided into two 7½-minute sections. For the first half, move your hands, palms up, in an outward circular motion. Starting at your navel, both hands move forward then divide to make two large circles mirroring each other, left and right. The movement should be so slow that at times there will appear to be no movement at all. Feel that you are giving energy outward to the universe.

After 7½ minutes, turn your hands palms down and start moving them in the opposite directions. Now your hands will come together toward your navel and divide outward to the sides of your body. Feel that you are taking energy in. As in the first stage, don't inhibit any soft, slow movements of the rest of your body.

Third stage: 15 minutes. Sit absolutely quiet and still. Your eyes may be open or closed, but you should try to keep your mind empty of all thoughts. As thoughts arise, and they will, you can make note of them, but allow them to quickly pass away and return your mind to the stillness.

—Osho, from *Meditation: The First and Last Freedom*

Nadabrahma for Couples

Osho has given a beautiful variation of this technique for couples.

Partners sit facing each other, covered by a bed sheet and holding each other's crossed hands, one on top of the other. It is best to wear no clothing. Light the room only by four small candles, and burn a particular incense kept only for this meditation.

Close your eyes and hum together for 30 minutes, and your energies will unite.

—Osho, from *Meditation: The First and Last Freedom*

Shiva Netra

This third-eye meditation is performed in two stages and repeated three times, for a total of six 10-minute stages (one hour).

First stage: **10 minutes.** Sit perfectly still in a relaxed position, and with your eyes softly focused, watch a blue light. You can create a blue light by using a blue lightbulb or placing a blue cloth over a lamp. (*Caution:* Make sure that the cloth doesn't get too hot or touch the bulb and catch on fire.)

Second stage: **10 minutes.** Close your eyes and slowly and gently sway from side to side.

Repeat both stages three times.

—Osho, from *The Orange Book*

Prayer Meditation

This merging with energy is prayer. It changes you. And when you change, the whole existence changes.

—Osho

It is best to do this prayer at night, in a darkened room, immediately before going to sleep. If done in the morning, it must be followed by 15 minutes of rest. This rest is necessary, otherwise you will feel as if you are in a drunken stupor.

First stage: Raise both your hands toward the sky, palms and head up, just feeling existence flowing into you. As the energy flows down your arms, you will feel a gentle tremor: Be like a leaf in a breeze, trembling. Allow it; help it. Then let your whole body vibrate with energy, and just let whatever happens happen.

Second stage: After 2 to 3 minutes, or whenever you feel completely filled, lean down to the Earth and kiss it. You will simply become a vehicle to allow the divine energy to unite with that of the Earth.

These two stages should be repeated six more times so that each of the chakras (points of spiritual energy in the body) can become unblocked. More repetitions can be done, but if you do fewer, you will feel restless and unable to sleep.

Go into sleep in that very state of prayer. That will help very greatly because then the energy will surround you the whole night and it will continue to work. By morning, you will feel more fresh than you have ever felt before, more vital than you have ever felt before. The whole day you will feel full of new energy.

—Osho, from *Meditation: The First and Last Freedom*

Gourishankar

This technique consists of four stages, 15 minutes each. Osho has said that if the breathing is done correctly in the first stage, the carbon dioxide formed in the bloodstream will make you feel as high as Gourishankar (Mount Everest).

The first three stages should be accompanied by a steady rhythmic beat, preferably combined with soothing background music. The beat should be seven times the normal heartbeat and, if possible, the flashing light should be a synchronized strobe. (You can purchase the music tape for Gourishankar from the retailers listed on page 230.)

First stage: **15 minutes.** Sit with your eyes closed. Inhale deeply through your nose, filling your lungs. Hold the breath for as long as possible, then exhale gently through your mouth and keep your lungs empty for as long as possible. Continue this breathing cycle throughout the first stage.

Second stage: **15 minutes.** Return to normal breathing and with a gentle gaze look at a candle flame or a flashing blue light. Keep your body still.

Third stage: **15 minutes.** With closed eyes stand up and let your body be loose and receptive. The subtle energies will be felt to move your body outside your normal control. Allow this to happen. Don't do the moving: Let the moving happen, gently and gracefully.

Fourth stage: **15 minutes.** Lie down on your back with your eyes closed; be silent and still.

—Osho, from *Meditation: The First and Last Freedom*

Mirror-Gazing Meditation

This is the meditation to uncover your original face. It lasts 40 minutes. You will need a mirror and a candle. Practice in a darkened room.

Close the doors of your room and put a big mirror just in front of you. The room must be dark. Put a small flame by the side of the mirror in such a way that is not directly reflected in it. Only your face should be reflected in the mirror, not the flame. Constantly stare into your own eyes in the mirror. Do not blink. This is a 40-minute experiment, and within two or three days you will be able to keep your eyes from blinking.

Even if tears come, let them come, but persist in not blinking and go on staring constantly into your eyes. Do not change your stare. Go on staring into your own eyes, and within two or three days you will become aware of a very strange phenomenon. Your face will begin to take new shapes. You may even be scared. The face in the mirror will begin to change.

But really, all these faces belong to you. Now your subconscious mind is beginning to explode. These faces, these masks, are yours. Sometimes even a face that belongs to a past life may come in. After one week of constant staring for 40 minutes, many faces will be coming and going constantly. After three weeks, you will not be able to remember your own face because you have seen so many faces coming and going.

If you continue, after three weeks, the most strange thing happens: Suddenly, there is no face in the mirror. The mirror is vacant—you are staring into emptiness. This is the moment: Close your eyes and encounter the unconscious.

You will be naked—completely naked, as you are. All deceptions will fall.

—Osho, from *The Ultimate Alchemy*, volume I

The Unwinding Meditation

This is a meditation for those who practice at night, just before going to sleep.

As you lie in bed, waiting for sleep, take a few moments to unwind, literally. Start thinking of everything you have done that day in reverse order. Begin with "I took a few moments to unwind. I got comfortable in bed. I went to bed. I put my pajamas on…" and so on until you reach the moment in which you awoke that morning.

Office Meditation

Office-hours stress can be counteracted with simple, yet effective, meditations. This is an intelligent way of taking care of yourself and putting an end to the pattern of receiving abuse through untoward situations that crop up in your work and of giving out abuse to others or to yourself. Be gentle, be patient, and find a way to disperse stress so that it does not harm you or others. Meditation in the office returns you to your wholeness and integrity.

You can do a simple Vipassana meditation (see page 222) during your lunch hour. It needn't take the full 45 minutes—even 20 to 30 minutes of this simple technique will energize and calm you. The tensions of the office will disappear or seem less vital.

Gibberish

This is a highly cathartic technique that encourages expressive body movements.

Either alone or in a group, close your eyes and begin to say nonsense sounds—gibberish. For 15 minutes, speak totally in gibberish. Allow yourself to express whatever needs to be expressed within you.

Throw everything out. The mind thinks, always, in terms of words. Gibberish helps break up this pattern of continual verbalization. Without suppressing your thoughts, you can throw them out, in gibberish. Let your body likewise be expressive in its movements.

Then for 15 minutes, lie down on your stomach and feel as if you are merging with Mother Earth. With each exhalation, feel yourself merging into the ground beneath you.

—Osho, from *The Orange Book*

Pondering on the Opposite

This is a beautiful and very useful method. If, for example, you are feeling discontented, ponder on the opposite.

If you are feeling discontented, contemplate *contentment*. What is contentment? If your mind is angry, think about compassion and immediately the energy changes.

Keep a statue of Buddha or a photograph of a beautiful place. Whenever you feel angry, go into your room and look at the Buddha or the picture. Suddenly, you will see a transformation happening within you. The anger will change: The excitement will be gone, with compassion arising. And it is not a different energy, rather the same energy as anger, only changing its quality and going higher.

—Osho, from *The Orange Book*

Writing Down Your Thoughts

One day do this little experiment: Close your doors and sit in your room; just start writing your thoughts—whatever comes into your mind. Don't change them, because you need not show this piece of paper to anybody. Just go on writing for 10 minutes, then read what you have written. You may think that this is some madman's work. If you show this piece of paper to your most intimate friend, he may also look at you and think "Have you gone crazy?" This writing meditation, however, will energize your creativity, freeing it for work on important projects.

—Osho, from *No Water, No Moon*

Meditation and Work

Whenever you find yourself in a bad mood in the morning, try this meditation before heading off to work. For 5 minutes, inhale and exhale deeply from your abdomen, making sure that you take in and let out as much breath as possible. Feel with each exhalation that you are throwing your dark mood out. You will be surprised that within 5 minutes you'll feel back to normal and your low will have disappeared—the dark will no longer be there.

—Osho, from *Don't Bite My Finger, Look Where I'm Pointing*

If you change your work into meditation, that's the best thing. Whatever you do can become meditative. Then meditation is never in conflict with your life. It is not something separate but instead a part of life. It is just like breathing: Just as you breathe in and out, you meditate also.

And it is simply a shift of emphasis; nothing much is to be done. Things that you have been doing carelessly, you start doing carefully. Things that you have been doing for some result can be re-evaluated. To work only for money, for example, is okay, but you can make it a plus phenomenon. One needs money, but it should not be an end in itself. If your work can also bring you many more pleasures, why miss them?

You will be doing your work whether you love it or not, so in bringing love to it, you will reap many more things that otherwise you would miss.

—Osho, from *Dance Your Way to God*

Kitchen Temple Meditation

Transform the time of preparing your meals into your evening meditation. Chop vegetables Zen-style. Be silent and mindful; concentrate on every movement of your hands—one action at a time, all the while breathing deeply in and out. Be slow and careful. Honor the spirit of the ingredients that you are chopping and thank existence for providing you with such beautiful abundance.

Osho's Meditations

If you want to find out more about Osho's meditations, order his books, music tapes, and CDs that contain the meditations found in this book from the outlets below.

For more information on Osho, please take a few minutes to visit the Web site at http://www.osho.org. This is a comprehensive Web site in different languages featuring Osho's meditations, books, tapes, and an online tour of Osho Commune International, Osho centers worldwide together with selections from Osho's talks.

New Earth Records
P.O. Box 3368
Boulder, CO 80302
Phone: (303)402-1016 or
(800)570-4074
Fax: (303)402-1018

Osho's Mail Order
1439 West Highway 89A
Sedona, AZ 86336
Phone: (520)204-5628
Fax: (520)204-0043
E-mail: oshos@sedona.net
Web site: http://www.osho.org/shop/
shop.htm or simply osho.org

Osho Viha Meditation Center
P. O. Box 352
Mill Valley, CA 94942
Phone: (415)381-9861
Fax: (415)381-6746
E-mail: oshoavi@aol.com

Publications Osho
1120 Paquette
Brossard, Quebec, Canada J4W 2T2
Phone: (514)672-0799
Fax: (514)672-8657

BIBLIOGRAPHICAL
REFERENCES

Blauer, S. *The Juicing Book*. New York: Avery Publishing Group, 1989.

Colbin, A. *Food and Healing*. New York: Ballantine Books, 1986.

Dogen and K. Uchiyama. *From the Zen Kitchen to Enlightenment*. New York and Tokyo: Weatherhill, 1994.

Elson, M. Haas, M.D. *Staying Healthy with the Seasons*. Berkeley: Celestial Arts, 1981.

Kabat-Zinn, J. *Wherever You Go, There You Are*. New York: Hyperion, 1994.

Kushi, M. *The Macrobiotic Way*. New York: Avery Publishing Group, 1993.

Moore, T. *The Re-Enchantment of Everyday Life*. New York: HarperCollins, 1996.

Osho. *Dance Your Way to God*. Pune, India: Rajneesh Foundation, 1978.

———. *Don't Bite My Finger, Look Where I'm Pointing*. Rajneeshpuram, Oregon: Rajneesh Foundation International, 1982.

———. *From Medication to Meditation*. Saffron Walden: C. W. Daniel Company, 1994.

———. *Meditation: The First and Last Freedom*. London: Boxtree, 1995.

———. *No Water, No Moon*. Shaftesbury: Element Books, 1994.

———. *The Orange Book*. Rajneeshpuram, Oregon: Rajneesh Foundation International, 1983.

———. *The Revolution*. Pune, India: Rajneesh Foundation, 1979.

———. *The Ultimate Alchemy*, volume I. Pune, India: Rajneesh Foundation, 1976.

Pitchford, P. *Healing with Whole Foods*. Berkeley: North Atlantic Foods, 1993.

Sato, K. *The Zen Life*. New York, Tokyo, Kyoto: Weatherhill/Tankosha, 1991.

Sharon, Dr. M. *Complete Nutrition*. New York: Avery Publishing Group, 1994.

Turner, K. *The Self-Healing Cookbook*. Vashon Island: Earthtone Press, 1987.

INDEX

Underscored page references indicated boxed text.

Nuts. *See also specific types*
  Apple, Celery, and Nut Delight, 104
  Brown Rice Porridge, 95–96
  Firnee, 105–6
  Nut Burgers, 203

Oat groats
  Fig and Oat Porridge, 95
Oats, 49. *See also* Oat groats; Rolled oats
Office meditation, 227–28
Olives
  Caper and Black Olive Dressing, 83–84
  Chicory and Bean Salad, 146–14
  Panzerotti and Glazed Beets, 175–76
  Potato Cakes with Spinach Sauce, 171–72
  Sprouted Lentil Salad, 142–43
  Stuffed Zucchini with Olive and Tomato
    Sauce, 124–26
Onions
  Basic Stock, 88–89
  Broccoli-Cauliflower Bake with Butter
    Beans, 158–60
  Cabbage and White Bean Soup, 187–88
  Cauliflower Béchmal with Baked Potatoes,
    214–16
  Celeriac Soup with Grilled Onions, 209–10
  Chickpea-Potato Casserole with Tangy
    Arugula Salad, 198–99
  Cornbread and Sautéed Vegetables, 213–14
  Green Bean Salad, 162–63
  Grilled Onions, 209–10
  Guacamole, 72
  Hummus, 71–72, 169, 185, 204–5
  Italian Bread Salad, 148
  Japanese-Style Tofu with Assorted
    Vegetables, 176–78
  Mediterranean Casserole and Greek Salad,
    136–38
  Mushrooms with Swiss Chard and
    Almonds, 188–89
  Nut Burgers, 203
  Potato Cakes with Spinach Sauce, 171–72
  Rice-Stuffed Squash with Tomato Sauce,
    173–74
  Salad of Broiled Summer Vegetables, 141–42
  Salsa, 73
  Savory Stuffed Tomatoes and Pureed
    Pumpkin, 152–53
  Spanish Rice and Crisp Salad, 178–79
  Split-Pea Soup, 210
  Tofu Cottage Cheese, 70
  Vegetable Rösti with Pan-Fried Artichokes
    and Mushrooms, 216–17

Warm Whole-Wheat Pitas with Beans,
    184–85
  Winter Vegetables in Oriental Sauce,
    212–13
Oranges
  Orange and Grapefruit Juice, 112
  orange juice, 110
Organic food, 29–30, 45
Osho's meditations, 230

Paella, 178–79
Pancakes, 98
Papaya
  Papaya, Banana, and Coconut Smoothie,
    114
Parsley, 117
  Pumpkin Seed Dressing, 87
Parsnips
  Carrot-Parsnip Cakes with Shallot-Plum
    Sauce, 206–7
  Split-Pea Soup, 210
  Winter Vegetables in Oriental Sauce,
    212–13
Pasta. *See also specific types*
  Kasha, Spinach, and Pasta with Steamed
    Beets, 196–98
  Pasta Primavera, 130–31
  Penne Bake with Broccoli, Sun-Dried
    Tomatoes, and Capers, 211
  Vegetable Mousse and Pungent Corn Pasta,
    154–56
Pastry
  Pie Crust, 90
  Whole Wheat Pizza Dough, 91
Pears
  Cooked Apples and Pears, 107
  Pineapple, Apple, Pear, Strawberry, and
    Raspberry Juice, 113
Peas. *See also specific types*
  Pasta Primavera, 130–31
  Puree of Beets with Vegetable-Rice Salad,
    157–58
  Rice-Stuffed Squash with Tomato Sauce,
    173–74
  Savory Flaked Puffed Rice, 102–3
  Spanish Rice and Crisp Salad, 178–79
  Split-Pea Soup, 210
  Tabbouleh, 164–65
Peppers
  Caper and Black Olive Dressing, 83–84
  Chicory and Bean Salad, 146–47
  Japanese-Style Tofu with Assorted
    Vegetables, 176–78